UNDERSTANDING THE
"WHY"
CHROMOSOME

Other Cathy® Books from Andrews and McMeel

UNDERSTANDING THE
"WHY"
CHROMOSOME

A *Cathy* Collection
by Cathy Guisewite

Andrews and McMeel
A Universal Press Syndicate Company
Kansas City

ISBN: 0-8362-0423-9

Library of Congress Catalog Card: 95-77578

6

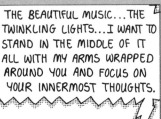

EVERY GIFT I'VE EVER GIVEN MY BOYFRIEND IS STUFFED IN HIS CLOSET.

THAT'S THE BEAUTY OF THE NEW COMPACT STAIR CLIMBER!

GIFTS FOR HIM

SEE? IT'S SMALL ENOUGH TO STACK RIGHT ON TOP OF THE ROWING MACHINE FROM 1989! THE 1991 TABLETOP POOL SET CAN LEAN ON THE INSIDE OF THE CLOSET WALL, BALANCED BY LAST YEAR'S ELECTRONIC PANTS PRESS MACHINE, AND STILL LEAVE ROOM FOR THE DESKTOP PLANETARIUM!

STUFF THE MINI PINBALL ARCADE, HYPNOTIC OCEAN WAVE STRESS REDUCER AND ALPHA-RHYTHM GOGGLES ON TOP AND ... VOILA! EVERY TIME HE OPENS HIS CLOSET HE'LL THINK OF YOU!

SOLD!

BEFORE WE CAN CAPTURE THE HEART, WE MUST FIRST TAKE OVER THE STORAGE SPACE.

NAH...I THINK I'LL WAIT UNTIL YOU SLASH THE PRICE EVEN MORE.

IF YOU WAIT ANY LONGER, THEY'LL BE GONE.

75% OFF

I'LL TAKE MY CHANCES. IT LOOKS LIKE YOU OVERBOUGHT.

THESE ARE FLYING OFF THE SHELVES! WE'LL BE SOLD OUT BY TONIGHT!

75% OFF

YOUR LEFT EYE TWITCHED WHEN YOU SAID, "FLY-ING"! YOU'RE DESPERATE! YOU'LL DROP THE PRICE!!

THEY'LL BE GONE, I TELL YOU! BUY NOW OR THEY'LL ALL BE GONE!!

RETAILING: ONCE, AN ART. NOW, A POKER GAME.

75% OFF

SOLAR-POWERED VENTILATED GOLF CAP...GOLF BALLS HAND-PAINTED WITH PICTURES OF THE PRESIDENTS...THE WACKY PUTT-MEISTER PUTT-MASTER...

FORE HIM

WAFFLE IRON IN THE SHAPE OF A FAMOUS GOLF COURSE... BUGS BUNNY GOLF BOOTIES... BOOK OF GOLF BLUNDERS... HILARIOUS SYNTHESIZED GOLF WISE-CRACK MAKER...

WAFFLE

GOLF MUGS, GOLF PLAQUES, GOLF SWEATERS, GOLF TIES, GOLF BOXER SHORTS...GIFTS THAT SAY WHAT'S SO HARD TO PUT INTO WORDS...

"I'M DESPERATE, AND IT HAS 'GOLF' ON IT."

BINGO. ALSO, "THANK YOU, GOD, FOR NOT MAKING HIM A BOWLER".

FORE HIM

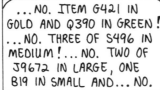

I WANT ITEM G421 IN BLUE!...NO. ITEM F8085 IN GOLD!

...NO. ITEM G421 IN GOLD AND Q390 IN GREEN! ...NO. THREE OF S496 IN MEDIUM!...NO. TWO OF J9672 IN LARGE, ONE B19 IN SMALL AND... NO.

FEDERAL EXPRESS THE ENTIRE CONTENTS OF YOUR CATALOG TO MY HOME, LET ME PICK THROUGH IT AND I'LL SEND BACK WHAT I DON'T WANT!!!

CLICK

WHY DOES EVERYONE CUT ME OFF JUST WHEN I'M READY TO MAKE A COMMITMENT?

WE SAID WE WEREN'T EX-CHANGING GIFTS THIS YEAR, CHARLENE.

I KNOW, BUT I JUST HAD TO GET YOU A LITTLE SOMETHING.

WE PROMISED WE WOULDN'T DO GIFTS, MARCIA.

I JUST SAW THIS AND THOUGHT OF YOU.

WE HAD A PACT, PAUL! NO GIFTS!

WE'RE SUCH GOOD FRIENDS...I COULDN'T HELP MYSELF!

ANOTHER BUSINESSPERSON, OVERWHELMED BY THE THOUGHTFULNESS OF OTHERS, FINALLY BREAKS INTO THE FESTIVE HOLIDAY SPIRIT...

IF ANYONE ELSE IS GIVING ME A PRESENT, SPEAK NOW BEFORE I MAKE MY LAST-MINUTE-MEANING-FUL-GIFT-PILGRIMAGE TO THE 7-ELEVEN!!

DO YOU HAVE ANY WRAP-PING PAPER, MOM? DO YOU HAVE ANY STAMPS? DO YOU HAVE ANY RIBBON?

DO YOU HAVE ANY GIFT TAGS? DO YOU HAVE ANY EXTRA CARDS? DO YOU HAVE A SPARE TOOTHBRUSH? ALSO, I FORGOT TO PACK PAJAMAS.

THE HEM TORE ON MY DRESS! MY DOG NEEDS A BATH! MY CLOTHES ARE ALL FILTHY, AND CAN I BORROW $30? THE CASH MACHINE WAS BROKEN!!

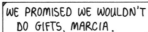

SIT DOWN, SWEETIE, AND LET ME FIX YOU A NICE, HOT CUP OF COCOA.

THERE SHE GOES, TREATING ME LIKE A CHILD AGAIN.

11

WE CAN'T CALL AUNT RENA AND WISH HER A MERRY CHRISTMAS UNTIL WE'VE ALL HAD A NICE, BIG SLICE OF THE NUTBREAD SHE SENT!

WE CAN'T CALL AND THANK THE STEVENS UNTIL WE'VE TRIED THEIR TIN OF CARAMEL CORN!

WE CAN'T CALL THE URBANS UNTIL WE'VE SAMPLED THEIR PECAN ROLL!

WE CAN'T THANK THE RIEMERS UNTIL WE'VE TASTED THEIR CHOCOLATES... AND THE MUFFINS FROM THE BAZELONS... AND THE CAKE FROM THE HERDEGENS... AND THE COOKIES FROM THE McNABBS!

SHOULD WE TRY THE EXERCISE TAPE BEFORE THANKING THE TUROFFS?

NO NEED. WE CAN SEE HOW GREAT IT WILL BE BY LOOKING AT THE BOX.

I CLIPPED THIS ARTICLE ON CANINE GUM DISEASE FOR YOU, CATHY.

THANKS, MOM. THAT LOOKS INTERESTING.

REALLY ?? YOU'RE READING SOMETHING I CLIPPED ??... WAIT. HERE'S A PIECE ON KEEPING PRODUCE FRESH...

THANKS, MOM.

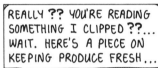

HERE'S ONE ON SETTING UP A COUPON FILE...

UH, HUH...

HERE'S ONE ON BUDGET MANAGEMENT FOR SINGLES... HERE'S ONE ON OFFICE ETIQUETTE... HERE'S ONE ON NEW WAYS TO FIND A HUSBAND... HERE'S ONE ON CHILDBIRTH AFTER AGE...

ENOUGH!!

WHAT'S A MOTHER FOR IF NOT TO PUSH THEM TO THEIR LIMITS?

HERE'S ONE ON COPING WITH YOUR MOTHER DURING THE HOLIDAYS.

♪ ROCK-A-BYE BABY, ON THE TREE TOP... ♪

SING TO MY DOG ALL YOU LIKE, MOTHER. I AM NOT LISTENING.

♪ WHEN THE WIND BLOWS, THE CRADLE WILL ROCK... ♪

I'M NOT LISTENING! NOT HEARING! NOT AFFECTED!

♪ WHEN THE BOUGH BREAKS THE CRADLE WILL FALL!... ♪

AACK! THEY NEED A GRANDCHILD! I'M RUNNING OUT OF TIME TO GIVE THEM A GRANDCHILD!!

THE LULLABY: GRANDMA'S LITTLE WAKE-UP TUNE.

Panel 1: WE HAVE THE PICTURES... WE HAVE THE ALBUM... WE'LL SIT DOWN, MAKE OUR FAMILY CHRISTMAS ALBUM, AND BE DONE WITH IT!

Panel 2: SINCE WE'RE DOING IT SO EARLY, WE CAN WRITE CUTE SAYINGS TO GO WITH ALL THE PHOTOS!

WE CAN DO THE SAYINGS ON A COMPUTER AT THE COPY STORE SO THEY'LL BE IN BEAUTIFUL TYPE!

Panel 3: WE'LL MAKE A "SPECIAL THOUGHTS" PAGE WHERE WE EACH COMPOSE A LITTLE ESSAY ON WHAT THIS CHRISTMAS MEANT TO US!

AND BLOWUPS! WE'LL GET BLOWUPS OF THE BEST SHOTS!

Panel 4: WE'LL START TOMORROW WHEN WE'RE NICE AND FRESH.

IT'S AMAZING HOW LITTLE WE CAN DO WHEN WE PUT OUR HEADS TOGETHER.

Panel 5: FOR A FEW PRECIOUS DAYS A YEAR, IT'S AS THOUGH YOU STILL REALLY LIVE HERE WITH US, CATHY...

Panel 6: THEN I SEE CLOTHES I DON'T RECOGNIZE GO INTO A SUITCASE I DIDN'T BUY AND I KNOW YOU'RE GOING BACK TO A LIFE FILLED WITH PEOPLE I DON'T KNOW AND PLACES I'VE NEVER BEEN, AND IT HITS ME ALL OVER AGAIN THAT IT WILL NEVER BE THE WAY IT WAS, AND THAT THE HAPPIEST TIME OF OUR LIFE IS OVER FOREVER...

Panel 7: I'LL CALL EVERY DAY, MOM! I'LL VISIT EVERY WEEK! I'LL WRITE LETTERS AND I'LL SPEND MY WHOLE SUMMER VACATION WITH YOU!

Panel 8: HIT THEM WITH THE PLEDGE DRIVE WHILE THE DOCUDRAMA IS STILL FRESH.

Panel 9: THE $155 VELVET GOWN... THE $90 VELVET CLOAK... THE $80 VELVET SHOES...

Panel 10: THE $45 VELVET BAG... THE $35 VELVET CAP... THE $15 VELVET CHOKER...

Panel 11: PUT IT ALL TOGETHER AND WHAT DO YOU HAVE??

Panel 12: THE EXTREMELY EXPENSIVE NEW YEAR'S EVE DOG-WALKING OUTFIT.

Panel 1 (thought): CLEAR THE OFFICE AND BEGIN THE NEW YEAR!
Panel 1 (thought): NO, YOU IDIOT! NOT LIKE THAT!

Panel 2 (thought): JUST DEAL WITH THE PAPERS ONE AT A TIME!
Panel 2 (thought): DON'T START WITH THAT ONE! WHAT A MORON!

Panel 3 (thought): PERSEVERE! GO THE DISTANCE! JUST GET TO IT!
Panel 3 (thought): YOU'RE A FRAUD! A HOPELESS FRAUD!

Panel 4: HOW'S THE DESK COMING?
Panel 4: I WAS DOING FINE UNTIL A HECKLER BOOED ME OFF THE STAGE.
Panel 4: CLEAN UP YOUR OWN MESS

Panel 5 (thought): I CAN'T FILE THESE PAPERS FROM 1993 BECAUSE THEY'RE RELATED TO PAPERS I NEED IN 1994...

Panel 6 (thought): I CAN'T GET RID OF THESE LETTERS BECAUSE THEY'RE RELATED TO THESE PROJECTS... I CAN'T THROW THIS OUT BECAUSE IT'S RELATED TO THAT WHICH IS RELATED TO THIS WHICH IS RELATED TO THAT...

Panel 7: FINE! EVERYONE STAYS! EVERYONE STAYS AND YOU JUST HAVE TO LEARN TO SHARE THE SPACE!

Panel 8 (thought): I'M A 3,000-MEMBER FAMILY IN A ONE-PERSON CUBICLE.

Panel 9 (thought): OFFICE PAPERS NEATLY ARRANGED ON A SIX-PIECE DESK ACCESSORY SET THAT EXACTLY MATCHES THE FLECKS OF AMBER IN THE VASE OF FRESH LILIES ON THE DESK...

Panel 10 (thought): NEATLY PRESSED CLOTHES HANGING A HALF-INCH APART, ORGANIZED BY COLOR, OVER A BASKET OF FLUFFY MATCHING SWEATERS...PRISTINE BOTTLES OF BATH OIL LINED UP ALONG A SPARKLING TUB WITH COORDINATING LOOFAH AND ROBE...

Panel 11: I CAN BE THIS WOMAN! I HAVE IT IN ME! I'M SO CLOSE! SO VERY, VERY CLOSE!

Panel 12 (thought): ...ALL I NEED IS $4,000, THREE MONTHS OF SPARE TIME, AND SOMEONE WITH A BULLDOZER.

STEP 1: I SHOW UP AT CATHY'S WITH AN ARMLOAD OF PLASTIC STORAGE BOXES AND A CLIPPING ON HOW TO ELIMINATE CLUTTER.

STEP 2: CATHY SNAPS AT ME FOR TRYING TO OVER-SIMPLIFY HER COMPLEX LIFE.

STEP 3: I HIT HER WITH THE OLD, "SHE'LL NEVER KNOW WHAT IT'S LIKE UNTIL SHE HAS AN UNAPPRECIATIVE CHILD HERSELF."

STEP 4: WE ATTACK EACH OTHER'S UNFAIR ARGUING STYLES.

STEP 5: WE BEG EACH OTHER FOR FORGIVENESS AND HAVE A NICE BIG PIECE OF PIE.

STEP 6: WE RALLY TOGETHER TO BLAME THE FROZEN DESSERT INDUSTRY FOR RUINING OUR LIVES AND VOW TO SEEK REVENGE.

OUR HOUSES MIGHT BE A MESS, BUT OUR DISAGREEMENTS ARE FINALLY ORGANIZED.

I'M NEVER BUYING ANOTHER PIECE OF CLOTHING WITHOUT GETTING RID OF SOMETHING I DON'T USE, MOM!

THAT'S JUST WHAT I USED TO SAY TO MY MOTHER EVERY JANUARY, CATHY!

I'M NEVER LETTING OLD PAPERS STACK UP BECAUSE I'M NEVER DELUDING MYSELF THAT I'LL HAVE TIME TO CATCH UP ON THEM!

THAT'S JUST WHAT I USED TO SAY TO **MY** MOTHER!

I'M NEVER SHARING MY RESOLUTIONS WITH YOU AGAIN BECAUSE YOU ALWAYS SAY YOU USED TO SAY THE SAME THING!

THAT'S JUST HOW I USED TO LOOK WHEN I GOT MAD AT **MY** MOTHER!

MY GENERATION DOESN'T NEED VIDEOS OF OUR YOUTH. WE JUST CUE UP OUR DAUGHTERS.

SHAMPOO THAT MAKES YOUR HAIR GREASY... **THROW IT OUT!** CURLING IRON YOU TRIED ONCE AND HATED... **OUT!** ICKY MOUSSE, BAD GEL, GROSS COLOGNE... **OUT!**

ACKNOWLEDGE MISTAKES! ADMIT DEFEAT! GET ON WITH LIFE AND **GET THIS JUNK OUT OF YOUR HOUSE!**

... THEN I'LL SNEAK IT INTO THE TRUNK OF MY CAR AND DRIVE IT OVER TO **MY** HOUSE.

OUR FAMILY NEVER GETS RID OF ANYTHING. WE JUST RELOCATE IT.

19

THE SUPER SLIDE COMBINES LATERAL MOTION TRAINING WITH CARDIOVASCULAR CONDITIONING FOR LOWER BODY STRENGTH...

...WHEREAS THE DUAL-MOTION TREADMILL GIVES A COMPLETE WORKOUT WITH AUTO INCLINE TO 12% AND ADJUSTABLE UPPER BODY ACTION...OR, YOU MAY WANT TO COMBINE THE SIMPLE STEP BENCH TRAINER WITH A MULTI-STATION WEIGHT RESISTANCE HOME GYM!

OF COURSE, I CAN HELP YOU BETTER IF YOU TELL ME ABOUT YOUR CURRENT FITNESS REGIMEN.

I TOOK THE ESCALATOR INSTEAD OF THE ELEVATOR TO GET TO YOUR SHOP.

VERTICAL MOTION! LOVE IT! RIGHT THIS WAY TO THE ALPINE MOUNTAIN SCALER!

I WANT TO BEGIN AN EXERCISE PROGRAM, BUT I DON'T KNOW HOW TO START.

SIMPLE! START WITH STRETCHES ON AN EXERCISE MAT!

STRETCH AND THEN GO FOR A WALK. WALK WITH HAND WEIGHTS AND ELONGATED STRIDES, CHECKING YOUR HEART RATE EVERY FIVE MINUTES UNTIL YOU'RE PUMPING AT 75% CAPACITY FOR 20 MINUTES!

FOLLOW WITH 30 MINUTES OF WEIGHT RESISTANCE REPS ON THE PECS, BICEPS, TRICEPS AND ABS... 30 MINUTES OF STEP WORK FOR THE GLUTES AND QUADS... AND THEN EVERY TWO DAYS ROTATE IN RUBBER BANDS, FREE WEIGHTS, PUNCHING BAG AND JUMP-ROPE FOR THE FULL CROSS-TRAINING IMPACT!

SO MANY BEGINNERS MAKE THE MISTAKE OF SETTING UNREALISTIC GOALS!

PHASE ONE: I HATE THIS. I DON'T WANT TO DO THIS. I DON'T WANT TO BE HERE. I'M NEVER DOING THIS AGAIN.

PHASE TWO: I LOVE THIS! I FEEL FABULOUS! IT'S MAGIC! I NEVER KNEW IT COULD BE LIKE THIS!

PHASE THREE: WHAT'S THE POINT? WHY DO I TRY? IT'S TOO MUCH WORK! IT NEVER GOES ANYWHERE! I HATE THIS!

EXERCISE: FOR SOME, A LIFETIME RELATIONSHIP. FOR ME, A BLIND DATE.

← 1973 →
THE POWER SUIT.

← 1983 →
THE POWER SUIT FOR THE POWER BREAKFAST FOLLOWED BY THE POWER MEETING AND THE POWER LUNCH.

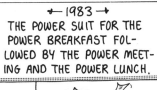

← 1993 →
THE POWER SUIT, POWER BREAKFAST, POWER MEETING, POWER LUNCH, POWER NETWORKING, POWER NEGOTIATING, POWER DINNER AND POWER NURTURING, ALL CULMINATING IN THE ALL-IMPORTANT POWER WORKOUT.

← 1994 →
THE POWER OUTAGE.

WOOF.

DRIVE TO WORK,
   DRIVE HOME FROM WORK...
EARN THE MONEY,
   SPEND THE MONEY...
FIX THE MEALS,
   CLEAN UP THE MEALS...

DAY AFTER DAY...
WEEK AFTER WEEK...
MONTH AFTER MONTH...
OVER AND OVER AND OVER
THE SAME SPIRIT-NUMBING,
SENSE-DULLING, ENDLESS TURF.

DESPERATE TO BREAK OUT OF THE DRUDGERY AND FEEL ALIVE, A NATION RISES UP WITH THE WEIRDLY POIGNANT RALLYING CRY OF 1994...

THIS YEAR I PLEDGE TO FIND TIME TO GO ON THE TREADMILL!!

I REFUSE TO BE PARALYZED BY ALL THE WORKOUT OPTIONS ANYMORE! I TOOK A SIMPLE STEP CLASS BEFORE WORK, AND I FEEL FABULOUS!

UH, OH. IF YOU DON'T DO WEIGHT TRAINING AFTER AEROBICS, YOU'LL LOSE MUSCLE MASS AS WELL AS FAT.

MUSCLE TAKES FEWER CALORIES TO MAINTAIN, SO YOU'LL REGAIN FASTER, AND IT WILL ALL COME BACK AS FAT!

NO! RESISTANCE WORK HAS TO COME FIRST, THEN A 20-MINUTE TRANSITIONAL STRETCH, **THEN** CARDIOVASCULAR!

NO! YOU HAVE TO PRE-EXHAUST THE LARGE MUSCLE GROUPS, OR INDIVIDUAL MUSCLE SCULPTING IS USELESS!

AACK!!

IF YOU FORGOT EVERYTHING ELSE AND JUST DID YOGA, YOU WOULDN'T BE SO SUSCEPTIBLE TO STRESS!

...AND BREATHE AND TWO AND BREATHE AND... WHAT ARE YOU DOING, ELECTRA?? NO STOPPING! NO SNIFFING!

...YOU'RE STOPPING AGAIN! WE'RE SUPPOSED TO BE DOING OUR POWER WALK! NO SNIFFING!

NO STOPPING, I TELL YOU! NO SNIFFING! HEEL! HEEL!

ANIMALS HAVE NO CONCEPT OF HOW TO EXERCISE.

HUMANS' NOSES ARE TOO FAR OFF THE GROUND.

I CAN'T GO TO THE GYM AFTER I GET HOME FROM WORK BECAUSE IT'S DARK OUT... THERE. I ADMITTED IT.

ME EITHER. I WON'T LEAVE THE HOUSE AFTER DARK.

EXCEPT FOR A MAN. I'D LEAVE FOR THE RIGHT MAN.

OR A CHOCOLATE FIX. I'D LEAVE FOR CHOCOLATE.

OR A SHOE SALE.

OR IF I RAN OUT OF MAKEUP.

I WILL GO OUT INTO THE NIGHT FOR A MAN, FOR FOOD, FOR CLOTHES, FOR MAKEUP, OR TO COMFORT A GIRL-FRIEND WHOSE LIFE HAS BEEN RUINED IN SOME WAY BY ANY OF THE ABOVE, BUT I WILL NOT LEAVE THE HOUSE AFTER DARK TO WORK OUT!!

WHAT'S NEXT ON OUR EXCUSE LIST?

CAN'T EXERCISE DURING LUNCH BECAUSE HAIR WILL GET ICKY.

IT TAKES 21 DAYS TO EMBRACE A GOOD NEW HABIT.

THAT'S ALL! 21 DAYS!

JUST 21 DAYS! IN THE GRAND SCHEME OF LIFE, WHAT'S 21 DAYS??!

...IT'S 20 DAYS, 23 HOURS AND 59 MINUTES LONGER THAN IT TAKES TO GET COM-FORTABLE WITH A BAD HABIT.

23

VIOLET THONG LEOTARD WITH MATCHING HEADBAND, SOCKS, SQUIRT BOTTLE AND TOWEL.

CHARGE IT UP!

POWER BENCH STEP WITH HANDBOOK, ANKLE WEIGHTS AND WARM-UP MAT.

CHARGE IT UP!

"BUNS OF STEEL."

CHARGE IT UP!

"FUNK'N'MOTION."

CHARGE IT UP!

"SCULPT AND STRETCH."

CHARGE IT UP!

WEEK TWO OF MY WORKOUT PROGRAM, AND I'VE ALREADY ACHIEVED MUSCLE TONE OF ONE WRIST.

YOU'RE ON YOUR WAY TO SEE A TRAINER AT THE GYM? WHAT DOES HE LOOK LIKE, CATHY??

I DON'T KNOW. I DIDN'T PAY ATTENTION.

HE MUST HAVE A FABULOUS BODY!

I DIDN'T NOTICE. HE'S JUST A KID WHO SHOWS ME HOW TO USE THE MACHINES.

A YOUNG, ATHLETIC MALE BODY LEANS OVER YOU AND GUIDES YOUR LIMBS WITH HIS MUSCULAR HANDS AND YOU DON'T NOTICE??

CHARLENE, I'M FINALLY DOING SOMETHING GOOD FOR MYSELF! DON'T RUIN IT BY TURNING IT INTO SOMETHING ELSE!!

TOO LATE. YOU'RE APPLYING MASCARA.

RATS. ONE LITTLE SUGGESTION AND AUTO-BIMBO KICKED IN.

I WOULDN'T HAVE EVEN NOTICED MY TRAINER WAS CUTE, EXCEPT CHARLENE TOLD ME TO NOTICE AND NOW IT'S ALL I CAN THINK ABOUT.

IT'S ALL I CAN THINK ABOUT SO IT'S RADIATING OUT OF MY HEAD, MAKING HIM KNOW IT'S ALL I'M THINKING ABOUT.

NO! NOT HIM! I DON'T WANT HIM TO THINK I THINK HE'S CUTE! QUIT RADIATING! QUIT SHOOTING SIGNALS! AFTER ALL THE MEN I'VE TRIED TO ATTRACT IN MY LIFE, DO NOT SEND THE CUTENESS SIGNALS TO THE TRAINER AT THE GYM!!

WOW! YOU LOOK FABULOUS TODAY, CATHY!

I'M LIKE A COLOGNE BOTTLE WITH A BROKEN SQUIRTER.

Panel 1:
I CAN'T GO OUT WITH A MAN WHO'S TEN YEARS YOUNGER THAN I AM! MY FRIENDS WOULD ALL TALK ABOUT ME, CHARLENE.

YOUR FRIENDS ALL TALK ABOUT YOU ANYWAY, CATHY.

Panel 2:
EVERYONE WOULD MAKE JUDGMENTS.

EVERYONE MAKES JUDGMENTS ABOUT YOU ANYWAY.

Panel 3:
THEY'D THINK I WAS SOME KIND OF PATHETIC ROMANTIC, CLINGING TO YOUTH BY GRABBING ONTO A DOOMED FANTASY WITH MY OLD, WRINKLY FINGERS.

WE ALL THINK THAT ABOUT YOU ANYWAY.

Panel 4:
HOW COMFORTING.

YOU MIGHT AS WELL HAVE SOME FUN. THE REST OF US ARE THOROUGHLY ENJOYING YOUR LIFE.

Panel 5:
YOUNGER MEN LOVE TO GO OUT WITH OLDER WOMEN BECAUSE OF ALL THE THINGS WE KNOW, CATHY!

Panel 6:

Panel 7:

Panel 8:
I KNOW HOW TO TURN A PERFECTLY HAPPY MAN INTO A CONFUSED, SHRIEKING LUNATIC.

BINGO! SEE?? THE YOUNG ONES CAN ONLY MAKE THEM WHIMPER.

Panel 9:
DID YOU GO OUT WITH YOUR CUTE TRAINER, CATHY?

DON'T BE RIDICULOUS, CHARLENE. I TOLD HIM HE WAS TOO YOUNG FOR ME.

Panel 10:
I TOLD HIM I HAD NO INTEREST IN SOMEONE WHO WORKS IN A GYM... THAT WE HAVE NOTHING IN COMMON... THAT I'M SEEING SOMEONE ELSE... AND THAT IT WAS A SIGN OF HIS IMMATURITY THAT HE WOULD BE SO UNPROFESSIONAL AS TO HIT ON A STUDENT!

Panel 11:
WHY?? DID HE CALL??

NO.

Panel 12:
MEN JUST DON'T KNOW HOW TO READ OUR SIGNALS.

DINNER WAS NICE, ALEX, BUT LET'S FACE IT, THERE'S NOTHING BETWEEN US. MAYBE I'LL SEE YOU AT THE GYM SOMETIME.

KISS

WILL YOU CALL ME? WHEN WILL YOU CALL? IF YOU CALL, WILL YOU CALL BECAUSE YOU REALLY **WANT** TO CALL? WHAT WILL IT MEAN IF YOU CALL? WOULD YOU HAVE CALLED IF ONLY I'D WORN CUTER SHOES TONIGHT?

MY LIFE IS A FAIRY TALE IN REVERSE. ONE KISS, AND THE PRINCESS TURNS INTO A TOAD.

IF I GO TO THE GYM, ALEX WILL THINK I'M GOING TO SEE HIM...OF COURSE, I AM PARTLY GOING TO SEE HIM, BUT I DON'T WANT HIM TO THINK I'M GOING TO SEE HIM...

...WELL, HE COULD THINK I **MIGHT** BE HERE TO SEE HIM, BUT I DON'T WANT HIM TO THINK I'M **DEFINITELY** HERE TO SEE HIM...WELL, HE COULD THINK I'M **DEFINITELY** HERE TO SEE HIM, BUT ONLY IF HE LETS ME KNOW HE WAS DEFI- NITELY HOPING TO SEE ME FIRST.

THE BALL IS IN YOUR COURT, ALEX! I AM ABSOLVED OF ALL RESPONSIBILITY!

NICE TO SEE YOU, CATHY!

KISS

AACK. BACK TO ME.

YOU SHOULD TRY THIS HAIRDO THE NEXT TIME YOU SEE ALEX, CATHY!

ARE YOU CRAZY? THE TIME TO EXPERIMENT WITH HAIR IS WHEN YOU'RE BE- TWEEN MEN AND FEEL WACKY AND DON'T CARE.

I'VE BEEN **KISSED**, CHARLENE! I CAN'T CHANGE ANYTHING AFTER I'VE BEEN KISSED!

I HAVE TO MAINTAIN MYSELF IN THE EXACT SAME KISSABLE STATE! **NO CHANGES!** I WOULD WEAR THE SAME OUTFIT EVERY DAY IF I COULD!!

SOME WOMEN KEEP A DIARY. I BECOME A TIME CAPSULE.

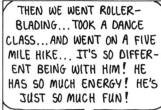

30

AEROBICS SHOES DON'T HAVE ENOUGH SUPPORT FOR RUNNING. DON'T YOU HAVE RUNNING SHOES, CATHY?

DO YOU HAVE WALKING SHOES?

CROSS-TRAINING SHOES?

NO.

NO.

NO.

WELL, YOU DON'T HAVE ANY SHOES AT ALL! COME ON! WE HAVE TO GO SHOE SHOPPING!

A MAN SAID "WE" AND "SHOE SHOPPING" IN THE SAME SENTENCE!!

WHO DID YOU JUST CALL?

CHANNEL 4. IT WAS A PUBLIC SERVICE ANNOUNCEMENT.

DO YOU...UM... HAVE ANY **CAREER** PLANS AFTER BEING A TRAINER AT THE GYM, ALEX?

OH, NO, CATHY! I LOVE MY JOB!

I GET TO HELP PEOPLE FEEL GOOD, AND I CAN TAKE OFF WHENEVER I WANT!

SUCCESS IS ABOUT BEING HAPPY, NOT MAKING A LOT OF MONEY! DON'T YOU AGREE?...CATHY??....

QUICK! THE HAMMACHER-SCHLEMMER MANEUVER! SOMEONE WAVE A CHARGE CARD UNDER HER NOSE!!

LOVE LIFE: AGE 5

HE'S PERFECT! I LOVE HIM!!

LOVE LIFE: AGE 20

HE'S PERFECT. I REALLY LIKE HIM.

LOVE LIFE: AGE 30 AND OVER

HE'S PERFECT, BUT DON'T GET EXCITED, MOM. HE'S TOO YOUNG. HE'S NOT RIGHT FOR ME. HE WORKS IN A GYM. WE HAVE NOTHING IN COMMON.

HOW QUICKLY WE GO FROM THE WONDER YEARS TO THE DISCLAIMER DECADE.

HERE'S MY PLACE, CATHY. MAKE YOURSELF COMFORTABLE WHILE I GET SOME COFFEE.

BRICK AND BOARD BOOK-SHELVES FROM COLLEGE...OUT!

HAND-ME-DOWN COUCH FROM GRANDMA'S...OUT! SPORTS POSTER FROM CHILDHOOD BED-ROOM...OUT! GARAGE SALE END TABLE...OUT! TACKY FIRST APARTMENT RUG.....

STOP IT! STOP REDECORA-TING! STOP PLANNING!! WHAT'S WRONG WITH YOU?! YOU HARDLY KNOW HIM!!

...HM! RATTY THROW PILLOW, COULD BE RECOVERED TO MATCH MY SOFA...

KISS KISS KISS

...WHAT'S THAT?

IT'S PROBABLY JUST MY ROOMMATE.

YOU HAVE A ROOM-MATE??

SURE! HI, KENNY! COME ON IN AND MEET CATHY!

OOPS. HI! I THOUGHT YOU WERE GOING OUT. I BROUGHT SOME BUDDIES OVER TO WATCH THE GAME.

HI!

HEY!

HOW'S IT GOING?

ANOTHER OLDER WOMAN TAKES THE PLUNGE: FROM SEDUCTRESS TO DEN MOTHER.

ALEX LIVES IN A CRUMMY APARTMENT WITH $75 WORTH OF FURNITURE AND A $15,000 SOUND SYSTEM...

HE HAS A ROOMMATE WITH A MOHAWK...A CD RACK FULL OF GROUPS I NEVER HEARD OF... AND HE HANGS AROUND WITH A BUNCH OF DATELESS BODY-BUILDERS WITH PART-TIME JOBS AT THE VIDEO STORE!

I'M A MATURE, INTELLIGENT, CONDOMINIUM-OWNING BUSI-NESS PERSON! WHAT AM I DOING GETTING INVOLVED WITH A MAN WHO GOES TO WORK IN TENNIS SHOES??!

HE'S ADORA-BLE AND HE WOR-SHIPS YOU.

WELL, THERE IS THAT.

LOVE CONQUERS MOST. EGO OBLITER-ATES EVERY-THING ELSE.

Panel 1: DO YOU THINK WE HAVE ANY FUTURE TOGETHER, ALEX? / I DON'T KNOW. WE'LL SEE WHAT HAPPENS.

Panel 2: WHAT DO YOU THINK YOU **WANT** TO HAVE HAPPEN? / I DON'T THINK ABOUT IT. LET'S JUST RELAX AND TAKE SOME TIME TO BE WITH EACH OTHER.

Panel 3: I RELAXED AND TOOK TIME IN MY LAST THREE RELATIONSHIPS! I'M OUT OF TIME, ALEX! MY TIME IS USED UP! I NEED TO KNOW EXACTLY WHAT'S AHEAD OR I NEED TO BAIL RIGHT NOW!!

Panel 4: AH, THE PASSION OF THE OLDER WOMAN... / HURRY! I FEEL MY FACE WRINKLING!

Panel 5: IF I'VE BEEN STRANGE, IT'S BECAUSE I'M AFRAID YOU'RE GOING TO LEAVE ME, ALEX. / I'M NOT GOING TO LEAVE, CATHY.

Panel 6: WELL, NO ONE **THINKS** THEY'RE GOING TO LEAVE, AND THEN THEY LEAVE. / WHY WOULD I LEAVE?

Panel 7: WHY DOES ANYONE LEAVE?? THEY JUST LEAVE! PEOPLE SAY THEY WON'T LEAVE AND THEN THEY LEAVE! THE WORLD IS FILLED WITH PEOPLE WHO LEAVE!! **DON'T LEAVE! SWEAR YOU WON'T LEAVE!!**

Panel 8: I HAVE TO GO NOW. / TALK ABOUT YOUR SELF-FULFILLING PARANOIA...

Panel 9: ALEX ADORES ME BUT... EH, I THINK I CAN DO BETTER. / OF COURSE YOU THINK YOU CAN, CATHY.

Panel 10: AS SOON AS ONE MAN LIKES YOU, YOU GET CONFIDENT THAT **ANY** MAN WOULD FALL IN LOVE WITH YOU... YOU START COMPARING WHO YOU'RE WITH AGAINST YOUR NEW FANTASY SUITORS...

Panel 11: ...THE MAN YOU'RE WITH DOESN'T MEASURE UP... YOU PICK HIM APART UNTIL HE DUMPS YOU... AND YOU END UP WITH NO RELATIONSHIP, NO SUITORS.... PLOPPED RIGHT SMACK BACK IN THE VAT OF INSECURITY WHERE YOU STARTED!!

Panel 12: DON'T HATE ME BECAUSE I'M DESIRABLE, CHARLENE. / HOMING INSTINCT OF THE TERMINALLY SINGLE.

WHOEVER HANGS UP FIRST WINS. IT'S JUVENILE... IT'S PETTY... BUT IT'S A CLASSIC COMPONENT OF THE TELEPHONE POWER DANCE.

THE ACTUAL CONVERSATION DOESN'T MATTER. ALL THAT COUNTS IS THAT YOU'RE THE ONE WHO WANTS TO GET OFF THE PHONE FIRST. THE PERSON WHO ENDS THE PHONE CALL WINS.

HELLO.

SLAM!

HAH!

CONGRATULATIONS.

I GOT HIS MACHINE. IT WAS A DRAW.

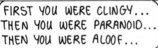
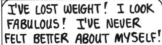

THIS SPRING, EVERY SINGLE ITEM IS MADE TO COORDINATE WITH SOMETHING YOU ALREADY OWN...

THANK HEAVENS.

...SKIN!

THE SKIN OF YOUR TAUT TUMMY...THE SKIN OF YOUR SCULPTED THIGHS...THE SKIN OF YOUR PERKY BOSOM ...THE SKIN OF YOUR FIRM LITTLE REAR! FASHION '94 IS ALL ABOUT SKIN! YOUR FABULOUS, FLAWLESS SKIN!!

THUNK.

QUICK! RUN HER CHARGE CARD THROUGH THE MACHINE BEFORE SHE COMES TO!

I CAN SEE RIGHT THROUGH THIS DRESS!

ISN'T IT FABULOUS??

THIS YEAR'S WISPY, TISSUE-THIN FABRIC LETS YOU PLAY PEEKABOO WITH YOUR BODY, WHILE ASSERTING THE CONFIDENCE, STRENGTH AND NO-NONSENSE SELF-RESPECT OF A WHOLE NEW BREED OF WOMEN.

TOP IT OFF WITH A SASSY HAT AND THIS SEASON'S MUST-HAVE ACCESSORY...

...A BACKPACK TO STUFF A SWEATSUIT IN IN CASE YOU RUN INTO YOUR MOTHER.

ALSO HANDY FOR MY PLANE TICKET OUT OF THE COUNTRY.

SPRING FASHION, 1994: THE CAP-SLEEVED, PUCKERED-FRONT BABY-DOLL DRESS WITH ANKLETS AND GYM SHOES.

THE LACY "MY FIRST SLIP" DRESS WITH MATCHING ANKLE-TIED BALLET SLIPPERS.

THE TINY SWEATER AND BOX PLEATED SCHOOLGIRL MINISKIRT WITH KNEE SOCKS AND TAP SHOES.

THE SALES STAFF PLAYING HIDE AND SEEK.

COME OUT COME OUT WHEREVER YOU ARE!!

FITTING ROOMS

BIKER SHORTS FOR WOMEN WHO DON'T HAVE TIME TO RIDE BIKES...TRACK SUITS FOR WOMEN WHO DON'T HAVE TIME TO RUN ON A TRACK...

APRON DRESSES FOR WOMEN WHO DON'T HAVE TIME TO COOK... HOT PANTS FOR WOMEN WHO DON'T HAVE TIME TO DATE...

IT'S A LOOK THAT'S DEFINING A DECADE!

DENIAL WEAR.

HOW ABOUT A CUTE HOSTESS GOWN FOR THE PARTY YOU DON'T HAVE TIME TO THROW?

AFTER LAST YEAR'S DREARY GRUNGE LOOK, THE FASHION INDUSTRY HAS FINALLY DESIGNED CLOTHES FOR WHO WOMEN REALLY ARE IN THE '90s...

WE'RE FUN! WE'RE FLIRTY! WE'RE FEMININE! WE'RE FREE!

THERE ISN'T ONE THING IN YOUR STORE ANYONE COULD WEAR TO THE OFFICE.

NOT AN ISSUE. WE'RE UNEMPLOYED.

AH. GOOD THING THE TANK TOP ONLY COSTS $140.

SEASON AFTER SEASON MY SHOP HAS BEEN EMPTY. NO CUSTOMERS. NO SALES.

...AND NOW THE SHOPPERS ARE COMING BACK! THE FLIRTY MINIS AND SEE-THROUGH VESTS HAVE BROUGHT THEM BACK! THE BOXER SHORTS WITH CORSET TOPS HAVE BROUGHT THEM BACK! THEY'RE LOOKING! THEY'RE TRYING! THEY'RE...

BLEAH!!

THE DROUGHT IS OVER! THE PLAGUE HAS BEGUN!

39

THIS WOULD LOOK GREAT WITH MY CHUNKY PLATFORM CLOGS!

OH, DEAR, NO! THE HEAVY FOOT IS OUT!

LAST YEAR YOU SAID FLOWY FABRICS HAD TO BE GROUNDED WITH THE HEAVY FOOT.

WE WERE WRONG. FLOWY FABRICS NEED THE **LIGHT** FOOT.

ALL THE SHOES YOU BOUGHT LAST YEAR ARE WRONG, BUT THIS YEAR WE HAVE IT RIGHT! THE DAINTY LACE-UP FLAT WILL LAST FOREVER!

MAY I HELP YOU?

YES. DRESS MY FEET FOR THEIR NEXT LEAP OF FAITH.

SHOES

THIS MIGHT LOOK OK IF I WORE IT WITH SOME BIG JEWELRY.

BIG JEWELRY IS OUT.

BUT IT'S JUST ME IN A DRESS. IT NEEDS SOMETHING BESIDES ME IN A DRESS!

JEWELRY IS OUT. MAKEUP IS OUT. EXTERIOR FUSSINESS IS OUT.

TODAY'S ACCESSORY IS WORN ON THE INSIDE, AND IT'S CALLED CONFIDENCE!

RATS. I BOUGHT THE WRONG ONE AGAIN. MINE IS CALLED DONUT.

I SPENT ALL WEEK SHOPPING, BUT ALEX WILL UNDERSTAND. I'LL TELL HIM HOW HARD IT IS FOR A SELF-RESPECTING WOMAN TO FIND CLOTHES IN A WORLD OF KEWPIE DOLL DRESSES... WE'LL DISCUSS THE DEEPER MEANING...

....THE SUBTLE SABOTAGING OF A WOMAN'S POWER BY THE MINISKIRT...THE UNDERMINING OF OUR FINANCIAL BASE BY CLOTHES SO SHEER WE HAVE TO BUY FOUR LAYERS JUST TO BE ABLE TO LEAVE THE HOUSE...

HE'LL UNDERSTAND WHY I SPENT ALL MY FREE TIME AT THE MALL, AND WHY I'LL NEVER GO THERE AGAIN!!

HI, CATHY. THIS IS TOM AND HIS GORGEOUS GIRLFRIEND, KIM.

PARDON ME. I HAVE TO GO SHOPPING.

THAT MUST BE MY ROOMMATE, KENNY, AND HIS FRIEND, SHAWNA. GO IN AND SAY HI.

YOUR FRIENDS ARE SO YOUNG, ALEX. I DON'T KNOW WHAT TO SAY!

SAY ANYTHING, CATHY! JUST BE YOURSELF!

PUT ON SOME CLOTHES, YOUNG LADY! SHAME ON YOU FOR OVER-PIERCING YOUR EARS! AND GO TO YOUR ROOM UNTIL THAT HAIR GROWS OUT, YOUNG MAN!

IT'S GETTING HARD TO BE MYSELF NOW THAT MY MOTHER HAS TAKEN OVER MY BRAIN.

CATHY'S IN MANAGEMENT AT A MARKETING FIRM SPECIALIZING IN DATABASE ANALYSIS OF FIELD RESEARCH...

SHAWNA DOES ACRYLIC NAILS AND TEACHES A STEP CLASS AT THE GYM.

CATHY'S BEEN ON BUSINESS TRIPS ALL OVER THE COUNTRY...

SHAWNA ROLLERBLADED ACROSS THE STATE LAST YEAR.

I'M SURE YOU'LL FIND LOTS TO TALK ABOUT WHILE KENNY AND I FINISH DINNER!

WANT TO SEE A PICTURE OF MY DOG?

YOUR DOG? THANK HEAVENS! WE DO HAVE SOMETHING IN COMMON!

SEE? IT'S TATOOED RIGHT HERE ON MY THIGH!

OF COURSE, IT'S WOMEN MY AGE WHO REALLY PAVED THE WAY FOR WOMEN YOUR AGE, SHAWNA. IT MUST BE INCREDIBLE FOR YOU TO FACE A WORLD WITH SO MANY NEW OPTIONS!

NO KIDDING. NOW WE WOMEN CAN USE OUR COLLEGE DEGREES TO BE UNDERPAID IN 100 DIFFERENT PROFESSIONS... NOW WE CAN WORK AND SPEND ALL THE MONEY ON DAY CARE, OR NOT WORK AND BE HOMELESS...

NOW WOMEN CAN DEMAND MORE FOR OURSELVES AND GO BANKRUPT IMMEDIATELY, OR CHARGE IT ALL AND BE SLOWLY STRANGLED BY 18% INTEREST!!

HOW'S IT GOING IN THERE, CATHY?

I'VE JUST BEEN SOAKED BY THE FOUNTAIN OF YOUTH.

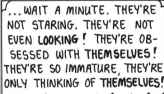

Panel 1: ALEX'S FRIENDS ARE STARING AT ME. THEY'RE STARING BECAUSE I'M OLD. STARING AT MY OLD FACE... STARING AT MY OLD LADY CLOTHES... ...THEY CAN'T BELIEVE ALEX IS DATING SOMEONE SO OLD...

Panel 2: ...WAIT A MINUTE. THEY'RE NOT STARING. THEY'RE NOT EVEN **LOOKING**! THEY'RE OBSESSED WITH **THEMSELVES**! THEY'RE SO IMMATURE, THEY'RE ONLY THINKING OF **THEMSELVES**!

Panel 3: WHAT ABOUT **ME**?? WHAT ABOUT **ME**, THE FOCAL POINT OF THE UNIVERSE??!!

Panel 4: ALEX'S FRIENDS ARE STARING AT ME...

Panel 5: IT'S 10:30. WE SHOULD GET GOING.

ME TOO... ...YAWN... IT'S SO LATE!

Panel 6: GREAT! COME WITH US. WE'RE GOING TO TRY THE NEW DANCE CLUB ON LIDO STREET!

NOW?? YOU'RE GOING THERE NOW??

Panel 7: OH, NO! WE'RE GOING TO GO WORKOUT FIRST AND THEN MAYBE HANG OUT AT A COFFEE HOUSE. THE DANCE PLACE DOESN'T GET GOING UNTIL AFTER MIDNIGHT!

Panel 8: I'M NOT ONLY IN ANOTHER AGE BRACKET, I'M IN ANOTHER TIME ZONE.

Panel 9: ALEX IS TEN YEARS YOUNGER AND WORKS IN A GYM, MOM.

DO YOU THINK YOU TWO WILL EVER GET MARRIED?

Panel 10: ONE OF HIS FRIENDS HAS A MOHAWK, AND ANOTHER HAS A TATTOO OF A SCHNAUZER ON HER THIGH.

BUT DO YOU THINK YOU'LL EVER GET MARRIED?

Panel 11: THEY WEAR CLOTHES I DON'T LIKE, LAUGH AT JOKES I DON'T GET, AND LISTEN TO MUSIC THAT GIVES ME A HEADACHE!

DO YOU THINK YOU'LL EVER GET MARRIED?

Panel 12: THE BIFOCAL VIEW OF LIFE: BLIND TO THE LITTLE DETAILS, CRYSTAL CLEAR ON THE DISTANT GOAL.

WANT ME TO GET YOUR PHONE, CATHY?

SURE, ALEX. WHY NOT?

RING RING

MAYBE IT WILL BE IRVING... ...HA, HA! TOO BAD, IRVING! THERE'S ANOTHER MAN HERE AND HE HAS FULL PHONE PRIVILEGES!

MAYBE IT WILL BE BRADLEY! ...HA, HA! TOO BAD, BRADLEY! YOU LOSE!!

IT WAS YOUR PARENTS. I INVITED THEM TO JOIN US FOR DINNER TONIGHT.

WHY ARE MOTHERS THE ONLY ONES WHO KNOW TO CALL AT THE WRONG TIME...

AN HOUR?!! YOU INVITED MY PARENTS TO COME MEET YOU FOR THE FIRST TIME IN AN HOUR??!!

DON'T WORRY, CATHY. I INVITED THEM. I'LL RUN OUT TO THE STORE, BUY GROCERIES, RUN BACK, COOK DINNER, SET THE TABLE AND STRAIGHTEN UP YOUR HOUSE.

YOU JUST SIT HERE IN THIS NICE CHAIR AND WORK YOURSELF UP INTO A PSYCHOTIC FRENZY.

OH, SURE! LEAVE ME WITH THE HARD PART!!

LIPSTICK! LIPSTICK! I DIDN'T BRING THE RIGHT LIPSTICK!

WE'RE JUST HAVING DINNER WITH CATHY AND HER NEW BOYFRIEND, DEAR.

WHY DIDN'T I WASH MY HAIR TODAY? WHY? WHY? WHY??!

IT'S JUST A FRIENDLY LITTLE GET-TOGETHER.

MY HAIR IS WRONG! MY DRESS IS WRONG! IT'S ALL WRONG!!

WE'RE GOING THERE TO MEET HIM. WHAT ARE YOU SO WORRIED ABOUT?

I HAVE TO BE SURE I'M ACCEPTED BEFORE I CAN REJECT ANYBODY.

OF **COURSE** I BROUGHT ANXIETIES FROM PAST RELATIONSHIPS TO THIS RELATIONSHIP, ALEX. DIDN'T YOU BRING ALL YOUR OLD STUFF, TOO?

WHAT STUFF?

THE INSECURITIES...THE NEUROSES...**ALL** THE OLD STUFF. THE STUFF THAT DOESN'T EVEN FIT ANYMORE BUT YOU CARRY IT ANYWAY JUST IN CASE... THE ICKY STUFF THAT WEIGHS DOWN YOUR BRAIN JUST WAITING FOR A CHANCE TO LEAP OUT AND MOW DOWN EVERYTHING IN ITS PATH.

THAT STUFF.

I DON'T REALLY HAVE ANY STUFF.

EMBARRASSING THOUGH IT MAY BE TO BE HAULING 100 TIMES THE BAGGAGE, I REMAIN SMUG THAT I'M TRAVELLING BETTER PREPARED.

46

$85.00... CONCERT TICKETS, BOUGHT TO SURPRISE IRVING...

$35.92... EYESHADOW SET, BOUGHT TO HYPNOTIZE IRVING...

$178.40... CHIFFON SKIRT, BOUGHT TO GO DANCING WITH IRVING...

$136.28... TAN PUMPS, BOUGHT FOR WHAT WOULD BE MY LAST DATE WITH IRVING...

A THOUSAND LITTLE HOPES SIGNED WITH A HAPPY LITTLE HAND... EACH ONE CALLING UP A WAVE OF MEMORIES AS CLEAR AS THE MOMENT ITSELF...

GRANDMA HAD HER SCRAPBOOK OF PRESSED ROSES... I HAVE MY BOOT BOX STUFFED WITH CHARGE CARD RECEIPTS.

EVERYBODY HATES ME! THEY HIRE ME TO DO THE JOB THEY HATE DOING MOST, AND THEN THEY ALL HATE ME ANYWAY!

THEY HATE ME FOR KNOWING THEIR SECRETS. THEY HATE ME FOR UNDERSTANDING THE FORMS.

ACCOUNTANT

I SPEND MONTHS SQUINTING AT A SCREEN FULL OF BEANSY, BORING NUMBERS, AND WHEN I FINALLY HAVE HUMAN CONTACT WITH MY CLIENTS, THEY HATE ME!!

HE'S BEEN A LITTLE EMOTIONAL SINCE HE HIT THE 39.6% BRACKET THIS YEAR.

I HATE YOU.

THE THANKS I GET FOR TRYING TO SHOW MY WARM, HUMAN SIDE.

ALL THESE RECEIPTS PERTAIN TO A RELATIONSHIP THAT DIDN'T WORK. HOW MUCH CAN I CLAIM AS A LOSS?

ZERO.

ACCOUNTANT

THE GOVERNMENT FROWNS ON SINGLE PEOPLE. HAVEN'T YOU BEEN PAYING ATTENTION?? THE HAPPY FAMILY UNIT IS "IN"! THE LONG-TERM COMMITMENT IS "IN"!

WITH THE REFORM OF THE TAX LAWS, THE GOVERNMENT PUT ITS FINAL, STAR-SPANGLED BLESSING ON THE SACRED INSTITUTION OF MARRIAGE!

LET ME GUESS ...TAX RATES FOR MARRIED PEOPLE JUST WENT UP AGAIN?

JUST CALL US A COUNTRY THAT CHERISHES OUR FAMILY VALUES.

ACCOUNTANT

49

I HAVEN'T CALLED IRVING IN THREE MONTHS, CHARLENE! I HAVEN'T CALLED IRVING BECAUSE I'M HAPPY WITH ALEX!

OF COURSE, IRVING HASN'T CALLED ME, EITHER. MAYBE HE'S HAPPY WITH SOMEONE ELSE, TOO. MAYBE HE'S HAPPIER WITH HIS PERSON THAN I AM WITH MY PERSON.

COULD I STILL BE HAPPY IF I THOUGHT HE WAS HAPPIER? ...NO. HE COULD BE HAPPY, YES. BUT HAPPIER, NO! I DRAW THE LINE AT HAPPIER! HAPPIER IS COMPLETELY UNACCEPTABLE!!

THE IMPORTANT THING IS, YOU'RE NOT THINKING ABOUT HIM ANYMORE, CATHY.

RIGHT. WHAT A RELIEF. EXCUSE ME WHILE I GO AND DON'T DWELL ON HIM.

WHAT ARE YOU DOING?

WE'RE REMOVING YOUR PHONE AND TYING YOUR HANDS TO YOUR CHAIR UNTIL YOUR LITTLE SPELL PASSES, CATHY.

WHAT? WHAT'S GOING ON??

YOU MADE US PLEDGE TO STOP YOU IF YOU EVER STARTED TWITCHING TOWARD THE PHONE TO CALL IRVING.

THAT WAS MONTHS AGO! I'M OVER HIM!! I'M CALLING FROM A POSITION OF STRENGTH!

WE TOOK THE SACRED VOW, INCLUDING, "IGNORE ME WHEN I SAY I'M OVER HIM"!!

ONCE AGAIN, MY ONLY MOMENT OF REAL WEAKNESS WAS IN BLABBING MY RESOLUTIONS TO MY GIRLFRIENDS.

I JUST NEED TO CALL IRVING ONCE TO MAKE SURE THERE'S NOTHING THERE ANYMORE, CHARLENE.

IF THERE'S NOTHING THERE ON THE PHONE, I'LL NEED TO SEE HIM ONCE AND MAKE SURE THERE'S NOTHING THERE IN PERSON.

IF THERE'S NOTHING THERE IN PERSON, I WILL HAVE TO KISS HIM ONCE TO MAKE REALLY, REALLY SURE THERE'S NOTHING THERE... AND IF THERE'S NOTHING THERE WHEN I KISS HIM, I'LL HAVE NO CHOICE BUT TO...

THE FLINGING YOURSELF INTO THE CHOCOLATE CAKE APPROACH TO BREAKING UP.

MARRIED PEOPLE KNOW NOTHING ABOUT CLOSURE.

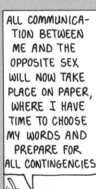

WHAT A DAY! I JUST WANT TO RELAX WITH A BIG BOX OF POPCORN!

52 GRAMS OF ARTERY-CLOGGING SATURATED FAT.

NO, ALEX. I'M NOT HAVING CANDY. JUST POPCORN. POPCORN IS INNOCENT!

A MEDIUM BOX HAS MORE FAT THAN THREE STEAK DINNERS.

SMALL POPCORN WITH NO BUTTER!

STILL HAS 19 GRAMS OF FAT. I CAN'T LET YOU DO IT, CATHY.

1994: THE YEAR WE BEGAN WEEPING BEFORE THE MOVIE EVEN STARTED.

IT'S ALL I HAD LEFT!!

SNACKS

POP CORN

WHAT HAPPENED? YOU WERE DOING SO WELL. YOU WERE LOOKING SO GOOD.

IT TOOK MONTHS FOR YOU TO GET BACK IN SHAPE... ...AND IN TWO SHORT DAYS YOU'RE RIGHT BACK TO WHERE YOU STARTED!

WHY CAN'T YOU LIVE IN MODERATION?? WHY IS IT ALWAYS ALL OR NOTHING WITH YOU??

HAVING NO CHILDREN TO FOLLOW IN MY FOOTSTEPS, MY DESK HAS BEGUN TO TAKE AFTER ME.

WHAT ARE YOU DOING, CATHY? IT'S ONLY 6:30.

I'M GOING HOME. EVERYONE ELSE WENT HOME AN HOUR AGO.

BUT YOU'RE A WOMAN! I COUNT ON THE WOMEN TO WORK EXTRA HARD TO PROVE THEIR WORTHINESS IN THE WORKPLACE!

I KNOW, MR. PINKLEY...BUT WORKING TWICE AS HARD TO TRY TO EARN THE SAME RESPECT HAS ONLY RESULTED IN MY DESK BECOMING THE DUMPING GROUND FOR EVERYONE ELSE'S PROBLEMS.

I DECIDED I'M SICK OF IT, AND THAT I, TOO, DESERVE A LIFE.

THE REVOLUTION IS OVER. THE REVOLT HAS BEGUN.

YOU USED TO BE AN OBSESSED, NEUROTIC OVERACHIEVER, CATHY... AND NOW LOOK AT YOU.

I KNOW, MR. PINKLEY. I'VE STARTED EXERCISING, EATING BETTER, AND LEAVING MY PROBLEMS AT THE OFFICE.

I HAVE LESS STRESS, MORE CONFIDENCE, AND FOR ONCE AM IN A HAPPY, HEALTHY, SUPPORTIVE RELATIONSHIP!

AHAH! I KNEW IT! WOMEN ALWAYS LET THEMSELVES GO WHEN THEY MEET A MAN!

YOUR NEW RELATIONSHIP IS HURTING YOUR PRODUCTIVITY, CATHY.

NOT TRUE, MR. PINKLEY. I JUST HAVEN'T BEEN WORKING EVERY NIGHT AND ALL WEEKEND LIKE I USED TO.

I STILL WORK JUST AS HARD ALL DAY EVERY DAY... BUT THIS IS WHAT'S LEFT TO DO IF I DON'T WORK AT NIGHT AND ON WEEKENDS.

INTERESTING, ISN'T IT? BY LOOKING AT THE VOLUME OF WORK THAT CAN'T POSSIBLY BE SQUASHED INTO NORMAL WORKING HOURS, WE SEE THAT MY JOB ACTUALLY REQUIRES THREE FULL-TIME PEOPLE!

NOTHING TRASHES MORALE LIKE PERSPECTIVE.

PEOPLE IN THEIR 50'S ARE BURNED OUT AND WANT TO SLOW DOWN, MR. PINKLEY...

CLEAN UP YOUR OWN MESS

PEOPLE IN THEIR 40'S ARE REASSESSING VALUES AND WANT TO SLOW DOWN... PEOPLE IN THEIR 30'S ARE SCARED THAT YOUTH IS SLIPPING AWAY, AND WANT TO SLOW DOWN...

PEOPLE IN THEIR 20'S HAVE SEEN WHAT WORKING SO HARD HAS DONE TO PEOPLE IN THEIR 30'S, 40'S AND 50'S, AND WANT TO SLOW DOWN.

JUST AS I SUSPECTED. THE ONLY PEOPLE MOVING AT FULL TILT ARE OVER AGE 60.

CLEAN UP YOUR OWN MESS

THE NEW FDA FOOD LABEL AND ITS IMPACT ON HOW AMERICANS EAT

BEFORE

AFTER

THE NEW FOOD LABELS MARK THE START OF A NEW ERA IN AMERICAN HEALTH. NO MORE DELUSION BY "LITE" MEALS THAT AREN'T REALLY LITE... NO MORE PRETENDING THAT "HEALTHY" SNACKS ARE GOOD FOR YOU...

NO MORE THINKING YOU'RE STICKING TO YOUR DIET BY EATING "5 CALORIES PER SERVING" POTATO CHIPS, WHEN IT TURNS OUT A "SERVING" IS ONE-HALF OF ONE CHIP.

WITH THE LAUNCH OF THE NEW "NUTRITION FACTS PANEL", PEOPLE CAN FINALLY GO TO THE SUPERMARKET AND GET THE INFORMATION THEY NEED MOST...

DO YOU HAVE ANY FOOD LEFT WITH THE OLD LABELS?

HOW COULD YOU BUY THIS STUFF, CATHY? DIDN'T YOU READ THE NUTRITION FACTS PANEL?

I GOT UP AT 6:00AM, ALEX... RACED TO THE OFFICE...

...KILLED MYSELF AT WORK ALL DAY... AND HAD 12 MINUTES TO HIT THE ATM, POST OFFICE, CLEANERS AND GROCERY STORE BEFORE CHARGING HOME TO CLEAN THE HOUSE, WALK THE DOG AND GET BEAUTIFUL FOR OUR DATE!

NO, I DID **NOT** READ THE NUTRITION FACTS PANEL! I GRABBED THE FIRST THING I SAW AND CONSIDER IT A MIRACLE THAT THERE'S ANY FOOD IN THE HOUSE AT ALL!

YOU WOULDN'T BE SO CRANKY IF YOU CHOSE FOODS THAT WERE HIGHER IN CARBOHYDRATE BULK.

PERFECT. I'VE COME TO THE LAST STRAW, AND IT'S MADE OF FIBER.

59

WINTER CLOTHES STORED?...NO. SUMMER CLOTHES READY?...NO. SPRING CLEANING DONE?...NO. VACATION PLANS MADE?...NO. GARDENING STARTED?...NO. HOME REPAIRS BEGUN?...NO.

DIET BLOWN IN ANTICIPATION OF SWIMSUIT SEASON?...YES.

THE DIET IS BLOWN! THE DIET HAS OFFICIALLY BEEN BLOWN!

EVEN WHEN IT'S SOMETHING REALLY HIDEOUS, IT'S A RELIEF TO HAVE ONE THING CROSSED OFF THE LIST.

I ATE A HOT FUDGE SUNDAE LAST NIGHT...SO WHAT??? IF I SKIP BREAKFAST AND LUNCH TODAY, I'LL BE EVEN.

IF I SKIP BREAKFAST, LUNCH, DINNER **AND** DO MY WORKOUT, I'LL BE **AHEAD**!...I COULD EAT A MUFFIN RIGHT NOW AND **STILL** BE AHEAD!...I COULD EAT TWO MUFFINS NOW, NOTHING FOR TWO DAYS, AND BE **WAY**, **WAY** AHEAD...

ON THE EVE OF BATHING SUIT SEASON, ANOTHER OVERACHIEVER FORSAKES A WORLD OF MODERN FITNESS EQUIPMENT FOR THE GOOD, OLD-FASHIONED "HOME GYM."

GOODBYE, TREADMILL. HELLO, VICIOUS CYCLE.

AS LONG AS I'M FASTING THE REST OF THE WEEK, I MIGHT AS WELL HAVE A BIG STACK OF PANCAKES!!

FEBRUARY 5: TRIED TO PROVE I COULD SURVIVE THE ADVANCED STEP CLASS.

MARCH 18: TRIED TO PROVE I COULD GO 35 MINUTES ON THE TREADMILL.

APRIL 11: TRIED TO PROVE I COULD STAND 50 WEIGHT-RESISTANCE REPS.

MAY 25: TRIED TO PROVE I COULD WALK PAST AN OPEN BOX OF CHOCOLATE.

IT ISN'T FAT. IT'S A SPORTS INJURY.

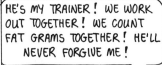
ALEX IS ON LINE ONE, CATHY!

AACK! ALEX! I CAN'T TALK TO ALEX! I'VE BEEN EATING ALL DAY!

HE'S MY TRAINER! WE WORK OUT TOGETHER! WE COUNT FAT GRAMS TOGETHER! HE'LL NEVER FORGIVE ME!

I'VE FORSAKEN OUR WHOLE HEALTHY RELATIONSHIP, AND FOR WHAT? CANDY I DIDN'T EVEN LIKE...COOKIES I DIDN'T ENJOY...CHIPS I NEVER REALLY WANTED....

SORRY, ALEX. YOUR GIRLFRIEND HAS JUST HAD A MEANINGLESS FLING WITH THE VENDING MACHINE.

I WAS DOING SO WELL ON MY DIET, AND I BLEW IT, ALEX! I'M SUCH A FAILURE! I'M SO HOPELESS!

EVERYONE DOES THE SAME THING, CATHY.

EVERY SINGLE PERSON ON EARTH IS IN SOME STAGE OF MAKING A BLUNDER OR RECOVERING FROM ONE.

IT'S WHAT BONDS THE HUMAN RACE. WE TRY...WE FAIL...WE TRY AGAIN. EVERYONE DOES IT, AND EVERYONE HAS FELT EXACTLY AS STUPID ABOUT IT AS YOU DO RIGHT NOW.

THE FINAL BLOW: ROBBED OF MY INDIVIDUALITY.

YOU'VE LOST SIX POUNDS LOTS OF TIMES, CATHY! YOU CAN DO IT AGAIN.

THAT'S THE PROBLEM, CHARLENE. I KNOW THESE SIX POUNDS.

EVERY TIME THESE SIX POUNDS COME BACK, THEY'RE STRONGER, TOUGHER AND MEANER....

JUST WHEN I THINK THESE SIX MISERABLE POUNDS ARE GONE FOR GOOD, THEY STAGGER BACK TO LIFE AND IT TAKES MORE AND MORE WORK TO GET RID OF THEM!!

MY FAT IS LIKE A STRAIN OF INSECTS THAT HAS DEVELOPED AN IMMUNITY TO BUG SPRAY.

SWIMWEAR: A MICROCOSM OF LIFE'S EXTRA LITTLE EXPECTATIONS FOR WOMEN

HIM:

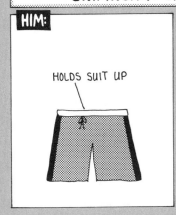

HOLDS SUIT UP

HER:

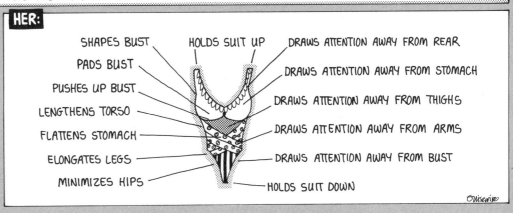

SHAPES BUST — HOLDS SUIT UP — DRAWS ATTENTION AWAY FROM REAR

PADS BUST — DRAWS ATTENTION AWAY FROM STOMACH

PUSHES UP BUST — DRAWS ATTENTION AWAY FROM THIGHS

LENGTHENS TORSO — DRAWS ATTENTION AWAY FROM ARMS

FLATTENS STOMACH — DRAWS ATTENTION AWAY FROM BUST

ELONGATES LEGS — DRAWS ATTENTION AWAY FROM BUST

MINIMIZES HIPS — HOLDS SUIT DOWN

FIRST, TRY ON THE MACRAMÉ THONG TO DULL YOUR SENSES.

THEN TRY ON THE STRING BIKINI TO KNOCK ANY REMAINING BRAIN CELLS UNCONSCIOUS.

YOU WILL THEN HAVE A FIVE-MINUTE WINDOW OF HORROR-INDUCED SHOCK IN WHICH YOU CAN TRY ON **THIS** SUIT WHICH, BY COMPARISON, WON'T LOOK THAT BAD!!

THE 1994 SWIMWEAR SALESPERSON: PART PERSONAL SHOPPER, PART ANESTHESIOLOGIST.

I'VE WORKED OUT FOR MONTHS, AND THIS IS THE THANKS I GET??

I'VE CLIMBED WHOLE MOUNTAINS ON THE STAIR MACHINE AND WALKED 10,000 MILES ON THE TREADMILL FOR **THIS**??

THIS IS HOW I STILL LOOK IN A BATHING SUIT??!

IMAGINE HOW BAD YOU'D LOOK IF YOU **HADN'T** WORKED OUT.

SAY WHAT THEY WILL ABOUT YOUTH, NOTHING TOPS THE PASSION OF THE MAINTENANCE YEARS.

MEN, WHO HAVE SKINNY LITTLE LEGS AND REARS, GET TO WEAR BAGGY BOXER SWIMWEAR.

WOMEN, WHO ARE GENETICALLY PROGRAMMED TO GAIN WEIGHT IN OUR LEGS AND REARS, HAVE TO WEAR TEENY SPANDEX SUITS.

THE SAME GARMENT THAT MAKES MEN FEEL MOST RELAXED PLUNGES WOMEN INTO THE DEPTHS OF SELF-CONSCIOUS INSECURITY, AND WE ARE SICK OF IT! JOIN ME, WOMEN! JOIN ME IN SPEAKING OUT AGAINST INJUSTICE!!

THEY'RE ALL TOO EMBARRASSED TO COME OUT OF THE DRESSING ROOMS.

WE SUFFER AS A GROUP, BUT WE PROTEST ONE AT A TIME.

IF I HANG ALL THE BATHING SUITS BACK ON THEIR HANGERS, THE NEXT ONE WILL FIT... ...IF I EXUDE A HAPPY, POSITIVE AURA, THE SUITS WILL WANT TO GO HOME WITH ME AND WILL TRY TO LOOK THEIR VERY BEST ON ME...

...THERE! SEE, SUITS? YOU'RE ALL ON YOUR HANGERS! I'M A HAPPY, POSITIVE PERSON! I'M A JOY TO BE WITH! I WILL NOW LOVINGLY SLIP INTO THIS SUIT, SLOWLY TURN AND...

AACKK!!

DIDN'T FIT?

DIDN'T LISTEN.

THIS YEAR'S SWIMWEAR HAS BEEN COMPLETELY REDESIGNED TO MAKE A WOMAN FEEL GOOD ABOUT HERSELF!

I LOOK BETTER WEARING NOTHING AT ALL THAN I DO IN THIS BATHING SUIT!!

TA, DA! WHAT OTHER PIECE OF CLOTHING HAS EVER MADE YOU FEEL LIKE THAT?!

65

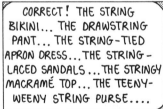

YOU FINALLY FOUND A BATHING SUIT, CATHY?? LET'S SEE!

I DIDN'T BUY IT, CHARLENE.

YOU SPENT FIVE HOURS TRYING ON A HUNDRED DIFFERENT SUITS, AND YOU DIDN'T BUY THE ONE THAT FIT?!

NO, I DIDN'T BUY IT.

I WANT TO MARCH INTO A BRAND-NEW STORE WHERE THEY'VE NEVER SEEN ME, PLUCK THE SUIT I KNOW THAT FITS ME OFF THE RACK AND BUY IT WITHOUT TRYING IT ON, MAKING SURE I'M WITHIN EARSHOT OF AT LEAST FIFTEEN CUSTOMERS!!

AH.

WE GET WHAT PLEASURE WE CAN OUT OF OUR SWIMWEAR.

BLEAH! I HATE SHOPPING FOR BATHING SUITS!

REALLY? YOU COULDN'T FIND ONE EITHER, SHAWNA??

NO! WHO COULD? THE STORES ARE FILLED WITH THOSE BORING ONE-PIECE SUITS! WHO WANTS TO GO BIKE RIDING OR PLAY VOLLEYBALL IN A ONE-PIECE?!

BESIDES, IT'S NOT LIKE WE ONLY NEED **ONE** BATHING SUIT! ALL **FOUR** OF MY FAVORITE BIKINIS FROM LAST YEAR ARE WORN OUT! I ONLY WORE THIS ONE DANCING ABOUT SIX TIMES, AND **LOOK AT IT!!**

...AND SO IT TURNS OUT THERE ARE THREE SEXES: MEN, WOMEN, AND YOUNG, SKINNY WOMEN.

BE TONED! BE FIT! BE TRIM! BE THIN! BE SHAPELY! BE LEAN!

BE TONED! BE FIT! BE TRIM! BE THIN! BE SHAPELY! BE LEAN!

BE TONED! BE FIT! BE TRIM! BE THIN! BE SHAPELY! BE LEAN.

WHY ARE WOMEN SO SENSITIVE ABOUT HOW YOU LOOK IN BATHING SUITS?

THE FINAL AND WORST COMMANDMENT: BE OBLIVIOUS.

Panel 1: MOM'S SINGLE TOO, CATHY. SHE OWNS A CONDOMINIUM JUST LIKE YOU DO, AND WORKS FULL TIME LIKE YOU DO.

Panel 2: SHE GREW UP WITH THE SAME VALUES YOU DID, THE SAME HEROES, THE SAME SOCIAL CHANGES... SHE EVEN PLAYS THE SAME GOOFY MUSIC YOU DO! YOU'RE PRACTICALLY THE SAME AGE!

Panel 3: THIS IS SO COOL! WHO WOULD HAVE THOUGHT MY MOTHER AND MY GIRLFRIEND WOULD HAVE SO MUCH IN COMMON?!

Panel 4: AACK!! YOU EVEN SOUND A LITTLE ALIKE!

Panel 5: I KNOW IT MUST BE HARD TO SEE YOUR SON WITH AN OLDER WOMAN. I THOUGHT ALEX WAS TOO YOUNG FOR ME AT FIRST, TOO.

Panel 6: BUT ALEX'S YOUTH HAS BROUGHT ME ALIVE! THE SPIRIT AND ENERGY AND PASSION OF SOMEONE YOUNGER MADE ME REALLY LET DOWN MY GUARD AND REMEMBER HOW TO HAVE FUN AGAIN!

Panel 7: I MEAN, YOU KNOW HOW HARD RELATIONSHIPS ARE. LOOK WHAT HAPPENED TO YOU AND ALEX'S FATHER.

Panel 8: HE DUMPED ME FOR A YOUNGER WOMAN. COULD THIS BE GOING ANY WORSE? NO. I THINK YOU'VE PEAKED, HONEY.

Panel 9: NO OFFENSE, BUT THOSE SHOES SEEM A LITTLE **YOUNG** FOR YOU. YES... WELL, THEY'RE NOT MY USUAL LOOK, BUT I THOUGHT THEY'D BE A FUN CHANGE.

Panel 10: OH? YOU CAST ASIDE YOUNG THINGS AFTER YOU'VE HAD YOUR FUN? OH, NO! I'D NEVER CAST ASIDE SOMETHING I CARED ABOUT! I'LL KEEP THEM FOREVER!

Panel 11: FOREVER? YOU'RE BASING YOUR FUTURE ON SOMETHING THAT SHOULD HAVE GONE TO A YOUNGER WOMAN IN THE FIRST PLACE?? I DON'T KNOW ABOUT THE FUTURE! I'M TAKING THE RELATIONSHIP ONE DAY AT A TIME!!

Panel 12: AHAH! THEN IT'S **NOT** THAT SERIOUS BETWEEN YOU AND MY SON! THERE'S NO PROBLEM SO BIG THAT IT CAN'T BE DISCUSSED THROUGH FOOTWEAR.

OH, ALEX, THAT WAS HORRIBLE! YOUR MOTHER MADE ME SO INSECURE!

...NO. SHE DIDN'T **MAKE** ME INSECURE. I **LET** HER MAKE ME INSECURE...NO. I DIDN'T **LET** HER. I ASSUMED SHE'D JUDGE ME, AND I MADE **MYSELF** INSECURE!!

I CREATED THE WHOLE INSECURITY MYSELF! I MASTERMINDED THE WEIRD-NESS! I AND I ALONE OR-CHESTRATED THE ASSAULT ON AND DESTRUCTION OF MY SELF-CONFIDENCE!!

I MAY BE A WIMP, BUT I'M AN OMNIPOTENT WIMP.

MARK CAN'T STAY LATE BECAUSE HE COACHES HIS DAUGHTER'S SOCCER TEAM.

I'M TRYING TO NURTURE A NEW RELATIONSHIP.

JULIE CAN'T STAY BECAUSE SHE HAS TO TAKE HER SON TO KARATE CLASS.

I'M IN THE FRAGILE FIRST STAGES OF ROMANCE!

PAUL CAN'T STAY BECAUSE HE HAS TO PICK UP HIS KIDS AT DAYCARE.

I HAVE THE EMOTIONAL EQUIVALENT OF A **SCREAMING**, COLICKY NEW-BORN IN MY BRAIN!!

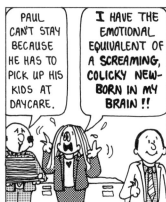

LOOKS LIKE IT'S UP TO YOU, CATHY!

NO ONE HAS ANY SYMPATHY FOR THE CHILDLESS MOTHER.

CATHY'S OVERWHELMED BY WORK, FRUSTRATED BY LOVE, AND FEELING THE FULL TRAUMA OF TRYING TO BE ALL THINGS TO ALL PEOPLE, AND NOT REAPING TANGIBLE SUCCESS IN ANY AREA.

SHE'S DESPERATE FOR COM-FORT, BUT HAS SOMEHOW MANAGED TO WAD HER UNEXPRESSED PASSION INTO A BALL OF BLAME, WHICH SHE WILL HURL AT ME, HER BELOVED MOTHER.

MOTHER!!

THAT'S THE BEAUTY OF LIVE THEATER...EVEN WHEN YOU KNOW THE PLOT BY HEART, EVERY PERFORMANCE IS A LITTLE BIT DIFFERENT.

MAIL TO ANSWER...
MEMOS TO READ...
REPORTS TO STUDY...
PAPERS TO ORGANIZE...
RECEIPTS TO FILE...
BILLS TO PAY...

WORKOUT CLOTHES...
AFTER-WORKOUT CLOTHES...
ACCESSORIES...
MAKEUP...
HAIR STUFF...
COLOGNE...

I HAVE BALANCE IN MY LIFE. TEN POUNDS ON EACH SIDE.

FOOTBALL'S OVER. BASKETBALL'S OVER. HOCKEY'S OVER. BASEBALL'S HALF OVER.

IT'S THAT BEAUTIFUL, ROMANTIC TIME OF SUMMER WHEN MEN TURN THEIR FOCUS TO ONE THING AND ONE THING ALONE....

WORLD CUP SOCCER!!

IS IT ME, OR DID THEY IMPORT A WHOLE NEW SPORT THIS YEAR JUST TO TORTURE US?

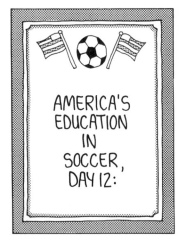

AMERICA'S EDUCATION IN SOCCER, DAY 12:

WHAT'S HAPPENING IN THE GAME, CATHY?

A BUNCH OF MEN ARE RUNNING AROUND AIMLESSLY AFTER A BALL.

NOW EVERYONE'S JUMPING UP AND DOWN. NOW I DON'T SEE THE BALL. NOW I SEE THE BALL. NOW I DON'T SEE THE BALL...

OH, FOR HEAVEN'S SAKE! WHAT'S HAPPENING IN THE GAME, KENNY?

A BUNCH OF MEN ARE RUNNING AROUND AIMLESSLY AFTER A BALL.

DO WE HAVE TO WATCH SOCCER AGAIN TONIGHT, ALEX?

OF COURSE NOT, CATHY. WHAT DO YOU WANT TO DO?

CLICK.

DON'T YOU WANT TO WATCH SOCCER?

SURE, BUT WE CAN DO SOMETHING ELSE. WHAT DID YOU HAVE IN MIND?

I WON'T BE HAPPY DOING ANYTHING ELSE IF I THINK YOU'D RATHER BE WATCHING SOCCER. I WANTED YOU TO WANT TO DO SOMETHING ELSE IN THE FIRST PLACE, BUT NOW THAT I KNOW YOU WANT TO WATCH SOCCER, I'LL ONLY BE HAPPY IF WE WATCH SOCCER.

YOU WANT TO WATCH SOCCER? OK.

IS THERE ANYTHING SO UNSATISFYING AS GETTING YOUR OWN WAY?

CLICK.

ELECTRA?? WHAT'S WRONG? YOU DIDN'T JUMP UP TO GREET ME!

I ATE YOUR BONE SANDALS FOR BREAKFAST.

ARE YOU MAD AT ME?? OH, DON'T BE MAD AT ME!

THE SANDALS WERE PRETTY GOOD, SO I HAD THE MATCHING PURSE FOR LUNCH.

I CAN'T STAND FOR YOU TO BE MAD AT ME! I NEED YOU TO LOVE ME!

I GOT THE MUNCHIES IN THE AFTERNOON AND SHREDDED ALL YOUR PANTYHOSE.

HERE! TAKE MY DINNER! I WANT YOU TO HAVE THE CHICKEN DINNER I BOUGHT FOR MYSELF!

IS THERE ANYTHING SO MAGNIFICENT AS THE HUMAN EGO?

I'VE BEEN SO PREOCCUPIED, ELECTRA, BUT I'LL MAKE IT UP TO YOU. I'LL MAKE TIME TO PLAY WITH YOU.

I MISS BEING WITH YOU... LET ME LOOK AT YOU... LET ME TOUCH YOU...LET ME HOLD YOU...

AACK!

HOW QUICKLY LIFE GOES FROM A WALK IN THE PARK TO A FLEA DIP.

FLEA DIP

73

MIRIAM: BONE TUNIC, BEIGE PANTS.

DENISE: ECRU TANK TOP, OATMEAL SARONG.

NAOMI: KHAKI VEST, CREAM CULOTTES.

ONE BLAND COLOR, CALLED A HUNDRED DIFFERENT NAMES, DEFINING 1994'S REBELLIOUS NEW BREED OF WOMAN:

ONE PROUD STALK IN A SEA OF WHEAT.

WHEW! I CAN'T BELIEVE WE DID THAT TO OURSELVES AGAIN, BRAD!

ME EITHER! HOO, BOY! I WAS WIRED!

HA, HA! I WAS BOUNCING OFF THE WALLS!

I WAS CLIMBING ON THE CEILING!!

AND THEN I CRASHED! WASTED!!

HOO, HA! COMPLETELY WASTED!!

THE NEW BRAVADO: WHO GETS MORE FLIPPED OUT BY A CUP OF COFFEE WITH CAFFEINE.

LOOK AT THIS MESS! YOU ARE NOT LEAVING THE HOUSE IN THIS CONDITION, YOUNG LADY!

WHAT'S ALL THIS? DID YOU THINK I WOULDN'T NOTICE IF EVERYTHING WAS STUFFED UNDER THE SEAT??!

OH, FOR CRYING OUT LOUD! I'LL CLEAN UP THIS ONE LAST TIME, BUT WHAT DO YOU THINK I AM...YOUR MAID??

WHILE THE WORLD RAISES ENLIGHTENED CHILDREN, I JUST TRY TO CONTROL THE TRIPLETS: MY PURSE, MY CAR AND MY DESK.

75

BORING COLORS.
BLAND FOOD.
BOTTLED WATER.
BOLTED DOORS.
BLAH COFFEE.
SAFE SUN.
SENSIBLE CARS.
FRUGAL SPENDING.
FLAT SHOES.

I CAN'T TAKE IT ANYMORE, CHARLENE! I'M SICK OF BEING SAFE!

I WANT TO BE DARING! GET CRAZY! I NEED TO FEEL ALIVE!!

SHE'S HEADING FOR THE HAIR SALON AGAIN! PLACE YOUR BETS!

FIVE DOLLARS SAYS SHE'LL CALL IN SICK ALL NEXT WEEK!

I WANT MY HAIR CUT OFF! CUT IT ALL OFF!

SORRY. WE INSTITUTED A MANDATORY TEN-DAY WAITING PERIOD AFTER YOUR PERM INCIDENT IN 1992.

TEN DAYS?! I NEED IT DONE NOW!

THE PERM INCIDENT WAS PRECEDED BY THE "HENNA" FIASCO, PRECEDED BY THE "THEY-SAID-I'D-LOOK-LIKE-KATHY-IRELAND-IF-I-HAD-BANGS" LAWSUIT.

NO ONE IN TOWN WILL TOUCH YOUR HAIR WITHOUT A TEN-DAY WAIT AND A NOTARIZED LETTER FROM A THERAPIST.

MOTHER!

THE SALON CALLED, DEAR. DAD'S LOCKED ALL THE SCISSORS IN THE FRUIT CELLAR.

I WANT SHORT HAIR, MOM! PLEASE! CUT IT ALL OFF!

YOU'D BE IN AGONY FOR FIVE YEARS UNTIL IT GREW BACK, CATHY.

THEN BLEACH IT! MAKE ME A CAREFREE, SUMMERY BLONDE!

YOU'D DIE OF EMBARRASSMENT, AND YOUR HAIR WOULD BE TRASHED FOR LIFE.

THEN PERM IT! YES! I'M READY FOR A PERM!

THE LAST TIME YOU GOT A PERM, YOU WORE A HAT FOR SIX MONTHS.

IF YOU WANT A NEW LOOK ON YOUR HEAD, WHY DON'T YOU JUST WEAR A HAT NOW??

A HAT?? OH, NO! I'M TOO SELF-CONSCIOUS TO WEAR A HAT!

I WANT SHORT, KICKY HAIR THAT SAYS I'M A SASSY REBEL, MOM!

YOU'RE NOT A SASSY REBEL, CATHY.

THEN I WANT WILD, FRIZZY HAIR THAT SAYS I'M DARING AND EXOTIC!

YOU'RE NOT DARING AND EXOTIC.

YOUR HAIR SAYS YOU'RE A NICE, HONEST, DOWN-TO-EARTH PERSON, WHICH IS JUST WHAT YOU ARE.

OTHER PEOPLE GET HAIRDOS. I HAVE A NUTRITION LABEL ON MY HEAD.

YOUR PROBLEM ISN'T YOUR HAIR, CATHY. YOUR PROBLEM IS YOU'RE TOO HAPPY.

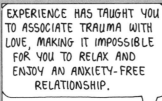

EXPERIENCE HAS TAUGHT YOU TO ASSOCIATE TRAUMA WITH LOVE, MAKING IT IMPOSSIBLE FOR YOU TO RELAX AND ENJOY AN ANXIETY-FREE RELATIONSHIP.

THUS, YOU WANT TO CUT YOUR HAIR OFF BECAUSE YOU'RE SUBCONSCIOUSLY HOPING THAT IF YOU CREATE ENOUGH MISERY IN YOUR LIFE YOU'LL BE ABLE TO FEEL REAL JOY AGAIN!

THE "ONE-TOO-MANY-POP-PSYCHOLOGY-BOOKS-BY-THE-SWIMMING-POOL" SYNDROME.

WAIT'LL YOU FIND OUT WHY YOU'RE WEARING THAT COLOGNE!

AACK!! I'VE BEEN BUTCHERED!!

WHY WASN'T I TOLD MY FACE IS TOO ROUND FOR SHORT HAIR?! I LOOK LIKE A BEADY-EYED CANTALOUPE!!

STICK IT BACK ON!! I DEMAND YOU GLUE MY HAIR BACK ON!!

OH, FOR CRYING OUT LOUD. SHE'S CHASING CATS IN HER SLEEP AGAIN.

WHAT A HORRIBLE DREAM! WHAT A NIGHTMARE!!

WHAT'S WRONG WITH ME?? A ZILLION PROBLEMS IN THE WORLD, AND I'M THRASHING AROUND IN MY SLEEP, DREAMING THAT I GOT A HAIRCUT!! HOW SUPERFICIAL CAN YOU GET?? HOW PETTY AND SELF-INDULGENT CAN ONE PERSON BE???

FROM THIS MOMENT ON, I VOW TO OBSESS ONLY ABOUT THE IMPORTANT, GLOBALLY SIGNIFICANT ISSUES THAT AFFECT THE LIVES OF ALL MAN AND WOMANKIND!!

I'M ALL OUT OF FAKE SWEETENER FOR MY COFFEE!!

CHOCOLATE, PLEASE.

LOW-FAT FROZEN YOGURT, FAT-FREE FROZEN YOGURT OR NON-FAT, NON-DAIRY DESSERT?

FLAVORS

NO FAT / LOW FAT / FAT FRE

NEW! 3 CALORIES

DONUT, PLEASE.

FAT-FREE MUFFIN, WHEAT-FREE MUFFIN OR ASPARTAME-GLAZED RICE PUFF?

DONUTS

ZERO FAT. NO CHOLESTEROL.

LOW SODIUM. LITE.

LEAN. LITE. LEAN. LITE.

FRUIT JUICE-SWEETENED.

QUICK DIET

FITNESS DIARY, JULY 16: EXPENDED 623 CALORIES TRYING TO FIND SOMETHING BAD FOR ME.

diet

I'M AT A TIME IN MY LIFE WHERE I LIKE A LITTLE **PAMPERING** WHEN I TRAVEL, ALEX.

ME TOO. I USED TO JUST LAY A BLANKET ON THE GROUND AND NOW I PREFER A TENT, CATHY.

CAMPING WORLD

WHAT I MEAN IS, I LIKE **MODERN CONVENIENCES.**

ME TOO! WHEW! LET'S TAKE BIKES IN CASE WE GET TOO TIRED TO HIKE!

I AM WILLING TO SPEND MORE FOR COMFORT!

ME TOO! I PAID $40 EXTRA FOR A BACKPACK WITH PADDED SUPPORT STRAPS!

...YOUTH! HOO, BOY! WHERE HAS IT GONE!?

IT'S OVER HERE, JUMPING UP AND DOWN ON WHAT'S LEFT OF MY GOOD NATURE.

Panel 1: I SEEM TO NEED A PAIR OF HIKING BOOTS.

A LITTLE LATE TO JUMP ON THE FASHION BANDWAGON, AREN'T WE?

Panel 2: THEY AREN'T A FASHION STATEMENT. I NEED THEM FOR HIKING.

THE HIKING BOOT WITH FLIMSY DRESS WAS OVER IN MAY.

Panel 3: IF YOU WANT TO THROW YOUR MONEY AWAY ON SOMETHING, THROW IT AWAY ON THE PLATFORM BASKETBALL MULE. IT WON'T BE PASSÉ FOR ANOTHER 24 HOURS!

Panel 4: NO, **REALLY!** I'M GOING **HIKING!** I NEED BOOTS FOR **HIKING!**

NO ONE EVER LIKES TO ADMIT SHE'S SUCCUMBING TO A TREND.

Panel 5: HAIR DRYER... HOT ROLLERS... STYLING WAND...TRAVEL IRON ...PORTABLE STEAMER...ELECTRIC PLAQUE-FIGHTING SYSTEM ...WHEW! I'M GOING TO NEED A BIGGER BACKPACK, ALEX!

THERE'S NO ELECTRICITY ON THE TRAIL, CATHY.

Panel 6: OH, I KNOW THERE ISN'T ANY ON THE TRAIL, BUT I'M SURE THERE'LL BE SOME WHEN WE GET TO THE PLACE.

THERE'S NO "PLACE".

Panel 7: DON'T BE SILLY! WE'LL GO IN SOMEWHERE AND ASK THEM TO SWITCH ON THE POWER!

THERE'S NO "IN". THERE'S NO "SOMEWHERE". THERE'S NO "THEM". IT'S JUST YOU AND ME AND THE WILDERNESS!

Panel 8: HELLO. I'D LIKE TO BUY A 150-MILE EXTENSION CORD.

Hardware

SPECIAL DRILL BITS

Panel 9: SEXY TOSS-ON LAYERED TOPS!

HYDROPHOBIC FABRICS TAKE REEKING SWEAT FROM BODY TO OUTER LAYERS.

FITTING ROOM

BODY GEAR

Panel 10: THICK, SCRUNCHY SOCK HIGHLIGHTS SAUCY CURVE OF THE CALF!

PROTECTS LEGS FROM DISEASE-BEARING TICKS.

FOOT GEAR

HEAD GEAR

STAFF

Panel 11: CHUNKY BOOT ADDS RAKISH ALLURE TO WISPY CLOTHING!

GUARDS AGAINST CRUSHED ANKLES AND NECESSITY OF ON-TRAIL AMPUTATION OF FEET.

HEAD GEAR

STAFF

Panel 12: COSMO WOMAN HITS THE SPORTING GOODS STORE.

HAIR SWEPT UP IN FLIRTY NEON CAP!

PREVENTS HUNTERS FROM MISTAKING YOU FOR LIVE GAME.

HEAD GEAR

SLEEP GEAR

STAFF

SIMON AND I SPENT LAST NIGHT READING ABOUT THE CHATEAUS WE'RE GOING TO VISIT IN FRANCE, CATHY!

ALEX AND I READ THE MANUAL FOR HIS NEW MULTI-FUEL CAMP COOK STOVE.

WE MAPPED OUT A WALKING TOUR OF PARISIAN BOUTIQUES!

WE PRACTICED DISASTER SCENARIOS, INCLUDING TICK, SNAKE AND BEAR ATTACK.

WE STUDIED FRENCH LANGUAGE TAPES IN BED!

WE DID AN HOUR OF HIKING-SPECIFIC WEIGHT TRAINING FOR THE QUADS AND HAMSTRINGS.

OUR CLOTHES ARE HUGGING EACH OTHER IN THE SUITCASE!

YOU'RE ALREADY HAVING A BETTER VACATION, AND NO ONE WENT ANYWHERE YET!!!

IN CASE OF CLIENT EMERGENCY WHILE YOU'RE ON VACATION, CATHY, I'LL NEED YOUR HOTEL NUMBER, FAX NUMBER, ROOM NUMBER, BEEPER NUMBER...

...CAR PHONE NUMBER OF THE CAB DRIVER FROM THE AIRPORT, E-MAIL ACCESS CODE AND, OF COURSE, THE DIRECT RADIO BAND LINK TO THE PILOT OF THE PLANE.

ANY OTHER SUGGESTIONS?

PLBTTT!

ONCE AGAIN, TECHNOLOGY FALLS A STEP BEHIND THE HUMAN SPIRIT.

HOW'S THE PACKING COMING FOR OUR CAMPING TRIP, CATHY?

TA DA! I HAVE ELIMINATED EVERYTHING BUT THE BAREST NECESSITIES FOR SURVIVAL!

THAT'S INCREDIBLE! YOU'VE MANAGED TO GET YOUR SUPPLIES FOR THE WEEK DOWN TO A 25-POUND LOAD!

THIS IS MY PURSE, ALEX. THE LUGGAGE IS OVER THERE.

I CAN'T TAKE YOU ON MY TRIP, ELECTRA, BECAUSE WE'RE GOING TO BE OUTDOORS THE WHOLE TIME... WELL, I KNOW YOU **LOVE** THE OUTDOORS...

BUT THE TERRAIN WILL BE ROCKY AND STEEP... WELL, I KNOW YOUR **ANCESTORS** WERE ROCK CLIMBERS...

BUT THERE WILL BE TOO MANY WILD ANIMALS... WELL, I **KNOW** YOU'RE AN ANIMAL, BUT...

I CAN'T DO IT, MOM. **YOU** EXPLAIN IT TO HER.

NO ROOM SERVICE.

SEE 'YA.

MY BOYFRIEND IS SEEING ME FROM THE REAR AND I'M WEARING SHORTS.

I'M OUT OF THINGS TO TALK ABOUT AND WE'RE ONLY ONE HOUR INTO A FIVE-DAY TRIP.

MY HAIR IS GREASY, MY MAKEUP'S SWEATY, AND I DON'T EVEN KNOW WHAT I'M DOING HERE. I'M TEN YEARS TOO OLD FOR HIM!!!

ARE YOU OK, CATHY?

DID WE BRING ANY INSECURITY REPELLANT?

LET'S HIKE UP TO THAT ROCK, CATHY.

YES! GET TO THE ROCK! HIKE, HIKE! HIKE TO THE ROCK!

WHEW! I WANT TO SIT AND RELAX FOR A MINUTE!

RELAX FOR A MINUTE! OKAY! ...58 SECONDS... ...59 SECONDS... ONE MINUTE! WE HAVE RELAXED FOR A MINUTE!

...NO. I MEAN, JUST SIT AND TAKE IN THE SCENERY!

TREES...CHECK! SKY...CHECK! MAJESTIC PANO- RAMA...CHECK! LET'S GO!

YOU'RE SUPPOSED TO BE LIS- TENING TO YOUR INNER CLOCK, CATHY!

IT'S BEING DROWNED OUT BY MY INNER FILOFAX.

Panel 1: NATURE PUTS IT ALL IN PERSPECTIVE, DOESN'T IT, CATHY?

Panel 2: SUDDENLY, THE LITTLE DAILY STRESSES SEEM SO INSIGNIFICANT. THE PRESSURES THAT CONSUME US SEEM SO PETTY.

Panel 3: YOU'RE JUST A MICROSCOPIC SPECK IN THE ECOSYSTEM, CATHY...A MINUSCULE, MICROSCOPIC SPECK...

Panel 4: ...HOLDING A TEENY, TINY CELLULAR PHONE.

WHAT DO YOU MEAN, YOU DON'T DELIVER HERE?! I NEED HAIR CONDITIONER, I TELL YOU! I NEED CONDITIONER

Panel 5: I'M ACTUALLY STARTING TO RELAX, ALEX.

I KNEW YOU WOULD, CATHY.

Panel 6: NO DOORS...NO LOCKS... NO ALARMS...NO SECURITY SCREENS...THERE'S NOTHING LIKE A CAMPSITE!

Panel 7: ALL WE HAVE TO DO IS HANG OUR FOOD IN A TREE TO PROTECT FROM BEAR ATTACK, FIX THE GROUND COVER TO SECURE OURSELVES FROM FLASH FLOODS, ZIP THE TENT FLAPS TO GUARD AGAINST SNAKE AND INSECT INVASION, AND REVIEW EMERGENCY PROCEDURES IN CASE OF LIGHTNING STORM.

Panel 8: WHEW. FREE AT LAST.

OH, AND SPEAK UP! IT HELPS SCARE AWAY DISEASE-BEARING RODENTS!

Panel 9: HOW SOON DO YOU WANT TO GET GOING, CATHY?

I NEED TWO HOURS TO HEAT ENOUGH WATER TO WASH MY HAIR, ALEX...

Panel 10: ...45 MINUTES TO DE-TANGLE IT SINCE I DIDN'T BRING CONDITIONER...30 MINUTES TO FIND THE FAKE SWEETENER THAT'S BURIED IN MY BACKPACK...20 MINUTES TO DRESS LYING DOWN IN THE TENT...AND FOR EACH LITER OF WATER YOU MAKE ME DRINK ON THE TRAIL, I'LL NEED FIVE 10-MINUTE LATRINE STOPS IN THE WOODS.

Panel 11: ...BUT FIRST I WANT TO SIT QUIETLY AND WRITE SOME SPECIAL THOUGHTS IN MY HIKING JOURNAL...

Panel 12: *Moronic things I've done in the name of love...*

LOOK AT THESE, ALEX!

I KNOW...I COULD STUDY THE GROUND OF THE FOREST FOR HOURS!

I COULD MAKE PINE NEEDLE BASKETS AND SELL THEM TO PASSERS-BY...COLLECTABLE FIGURES OUT OF TWIGS...LITTLE MOSS PIN CUSHIONS...NOTE PAPER OUT OF DRIED LEAVES...

WHAT??

I COULD OPEN A STAND! A LITTLE OASIS IN THE WILDERNESS!!

WHAT ARE YOU TALKING ABOUT, CATHY?!

SORRY, ALEX. IT'S GENETIC. IF WOMEN DON'T SEE A GIFT SHOP, WE CREATE ONE.

HOW CAN MY SHORTS BE TOO TIGHT?? I'VE DONE NOTHING BUT EXERCISE FOR FOUR DAYS!

IT'S A COMBINATION OF THE HIGH-CARBO FUEL OF OUR TRAIL MEALS, PLUS YOUR MUSCLES ARE GROWING AND EXPANDING!

WHAT?? MY THIGHS ARE GROWING?? ALL THIS TORTURE AND MY THIGHS ARE GAINING WEIGHT?!!

IT'S GOOD WEIGHT, CATHY! IT'S STRONG, HEALTHY WEIGHT!

TO DO WHEN I GET HOME: MAKE DISCLAIMER POSTERS TO HANG ON MY LEGS.

LET'S TALK ABOUT US, CATHY.

I CAN'T, ALEX. I DON'T HAVE ANY MAKEUP ON.

SO WHAT?

NO MAKEUP... FILTHY HAIR... ICKY CAMPING GEAR...

I'VE WAITED MY WHOLE LIFE TO BE WITH A MAN WHO INITIATED A RELATIONSHIP DISCUSSION, AND I AM NOT GOING TO PARTICIPATE UNTIL I'M WEARING CUTE CLOTHES, GOOD HAIR AND MY LUCKY MAKEUP!

WHERE DID THAT COME FROM??

THE EIGHTH GRADE. SOME DREAMS NEVER DIE.

85

THANKS FOR A GREAT TRIP, CATHY!

HOT SHOWER! HOT SHOWER! HOT SHOWER!

CLEAN CLOTHES! CLEAN CLOTHES! CLEAN CLOTHES!

BED AND TV! BED AND TV! BED AND TV!

HAIRDRYER! PHONE! COFFEE MAKER! MICROWAVE!

HAVING BONDED WITH NATURE, ANOTHER OUTDOOR ENTHUSIAST STRUGGLES TO RECONNECT TO CIVILIZATION...

MOVE OVER, ELECTRA. I CAN'T SEE MARY HART'S FACE.

HERE'S A PICTURE OF ME AT THE TOP OF THE EIFFEL TOWER!

HERE'S ME, LOOKING FOR MY CONTACT LENS IN THE WOODS.

HERE'S SIMON, BLOWING ME A KISS IN FRONT OF THE MUSÉE D'ORSAY.

HERE'S ALEX, PULLING A TICK OUT OF MY TOE WITH TWEEZERS.

HERE I AM, WRITING POSTCARDS AND EATING BRIOCHE ON THE BANK OF THE SEINE.

HERE I AM, SCRAPING FREEZE-DRIED STEW OUT OF MY SLEEPING BAG.

OH, FOR CRYING OUT LOUD, CATHY! YOU DID IT AGAIN!

CONTENT DOESN'T MATTER. WHOEVER GETS THEIRS IN A PHOTO ALBUM FIRST WINS.

I WENT INTO OUR CAMPING TRIP WITH A BAD ATTITUDE, A CLOSED MIND, AND AN AURA OF DOOM.

I WHINED AND COMPLAINED THE WHOLE TIME WE WERE GONE.

I WAS INSENSITIVE, INFLEXIBLE, SUPERFICIAL, STUBBORN AND CRANKY, AND HE SAID HE HAD A GREAT TIME.

WHICH IS MORE FRIGHTENING... THAT HE LIKES ME FOR WHO I AM, OR THAT THIS IS WHAT IT IS?

I RACED AROUND FOR TWO WEEKS TRYING TO GET AHEAD ENOUGH TO GO AWAY FOR A WEEK...

BANK

NOW I'M HOME. I'LL BE RACING AROUND FOR TWO WEEKS TRYING TO CATCH UP FROM BEING GONE FOR A WEEK...

ONCE AGAIN, IT'S TAKING FOUR WEEKS TO DO WHAT WOULD HAVE BEEN A WEEK OF THINGS TO DO IF I'D BEEN HERE TO DO THEM.

MY LIFE: HOME OF THE DAILY COMPOUNDED ERRAND.

SOME OF ALEX'S STUFF WAS IN MY BAG WHEN I UNPACKED FROM OUR TRIP... HIS STUFF WAS MINGLING WITH MY STUFF IN MY LUGGAGE, AND NOW IT'S IN MY HOUSE!

I'LL DISPLAY IT ON THE COFFEE TABLE...NO. TOO TROPHY-ESQUE...I'LL CASUALLY TOSS IT ON THE KITCHEN COUNTER ...NO. TOO OBVIOUSLY FEIGNING ALOOFNESS...I'LL JUST SPREAD IT AROUND THE HOUSE...LITTLE TOUCHES OF HIM IN EVERY ROOM....

RING RING

HI, CATHY. SOME OF YOUR STUFF WAS IN MY BAG. I'LL RUN OVER AND DROP IT OFF, OK?

MEN DON'T KNOW HOW TO ROMANTICIZE DEBRIS.

YOU'RE SLOPPY!

YOU'RE NIT-PICKY!

YOU'RE IRRESPONSIBLE!

YOU'RE OBSESSIVE!

YOU'RE IMMATURE!

YOU'RE OLD!

YOU'RE SHORT!

YOU'RE FLABBY!

YOUR NOSE IS WEIRD!

YOUR TEETH ARE CROOKED!

ANOTHER SENSITIVE COUPLE TOSSES ASIDE TWO DECADES OF LITERATURE ON COMMUNICATION SKILLS IN LIEU OF THAT OTHER BEST SELLER...

"ALL I REALLY NEED TO KNOW I LEARNED IN KINDERGARTEN."

PBLTTT!!

ALEX AND I HAD A FIGHT, AND SUDDENLY ALL I COULD THINK OF WAS HOW MUCH I WANTED TO SNEAK OVER TO HIS HOUSE AND LET ALL THE AIR OUT OF HIS TIRES...

I KNOW...HEE, HEE...OUT OF NOWHERE ONE DAY, I STARTED DREAMING ABOUT POURING CRAZY GLUE IN MY HUSBAND'S REMOTE CONTROL AND MAILING HIS GOLF BAG TO A PHONY ADDRESS IN EUROPE!

SOMETIMES I LIE AWAKE PLANNING HOW I'LL POP OUT OF BED IN THE MORNING, BAKE WALTER'S FAVORITE PIE, AND HURL IT RIGHT THROUGH THE SPORTS SECTION INTO HIS FACE!

AFTER A LIFETIME OF HOPING, A MAN IS FINALLY PRIVY TO THE SECRET FANTASIES OF WOMEN.

NO ONE BREAKS UP AFTER THE FIRST FIGHT, CATHY.

THEY DON'T??

NO! NEITHER ONE OF YOU CAN BE SURE THE OTHER ONE WILL SUFFER ENOUGH.

YOU HAVE TO KEEP THE RELATIONSHIP GOING LONG ENOUGH TO KNOW THE OTHER PERSON WILL BE LEFT IN MORE OF A WRETCHED EMOTIONAL WASTELAND THAN YOU...OTHERWISE, WHAT'S THE POINT?? WHY SPLIT UP UNLESS YOU CAN DESTROY YOUR LOVED ONE'S LIFE?!

THANK YOU, MRS. HAPPILY MARRIED WOMAN.

CAN I HELP IT IF I GET A LITTLE NOSTALGIC FOR THE OLD DAYS?

IT'S CLASSIC, CATHY. WHEN PEOPLE TRAVEL TOGETHER THEY SEE ALL OF EACH OTHER'S LITTLE FLAWS.

WE DIDN'T FIGHT UNTIL WE GOT HOME, CHARLENE.

AH, BUT THE IMAGES OF EACH OTHER'S ANNOYING PERSONAL HABITS WERE BEING RECORDED ON YOUR BRAINS.

EVENTUALLY THE IMAGES GET PROCESSED AND VOILÁ! YOU HAVE A REPUGNANTLY CLEAR PICTURE OF WHO YOU THOUGHT YOU LOVED!

MOST PEOPLE SEE IT WITHIN A MONTH AFTER THE TRIP.

JUST MY LUCK. WE TOOK OUR PSYCHOSES TO THE ONE-HOUR DEVELOPER.

WHAT SHOULD I DO ABOUT ALEX, CHARLENE?

GOOD QUESTION. IF I ENCOURAGE YOU TO BREAK UP, I'LL HAVE TO LISTEN TO YOU WHINE ABOUT TRYING TO MEET SOMEONE NEW AGAIN AND...NO OFFENSE ...BUT, HO-HUM!

IF I ENCOURAGE YOU TO MAKE UP, I'LL BE HURLING MYSELF INTO THE SECOND PHASE OF THE RELATIONSHIP, WHICH IS WHEN ALL THE ICKY STUFF COMES UP AND, FRANKLY, WILL TAKE TOO MUCH OF MY TIME.

HOW WILL WHAT I TELL YOU TO DO AFFECT **ME**?? HOW WILL IT INCONVENIENCE **ME**?? WHAT'S THE UPSIDE FOR **ME, ME, ME**??!!

OH, FOR CRYING OUT LOUD!

NO ONE HAS ANY COMPASSION FOR THE THERAPIST.

YOU TALKED TO ME FOR AN HOUR ABOUT MY RE-LATIONSHIP, CHARLENE.

THEN ANDREA TALKED TO ME FOR AN HOUR ABOUT MY RELATIONSHIP. THEN MOM TALKED TO ME FOR AN HOUR ABOUT MY RELATIONSHIP.

THEN I CALLED ALEX AND ASKED HIM OUT TO DINNER.

WHAT?? YOU CALLED HIM?? HOW COULD YOU CALL HIM AFTER EVERY-THING WE SAID TO YOU?!!

I WANTED TO BE WITH SOMEONE WHO WOULDN'T DISCUSS THE RELATIONSHIP.

LISTEN TO THE WARNING SIGNS! BAIL NOW BEFORE YOU GET TOO INVOLVED LIKE YOU'VE DONE BEFORE!

...NO! DON'T GIVE UP AT THE FIRST SIGN OF TROUBLE LIKE YOU'VE DONE BEFORE!...NO! DON'T BE TOO FORGIVING LIKE YOU'VE BEEN BEFORE!

...NO! DON'T BE INFLEXIBLE LIKE YOU'VE BEEN BEFORE! ...NO! DON'T OVERANALYZE! ...NO! DON'T WIMP OUT! ...NO! DON'T MAKE RULES!

WELCOME TO MY HOME: TEST KITCHEN FOR RELATIONSHIP BLUNDERS.

I'M TOO TIRED TO GET READY FOR BED.

IF I GO TO SLEEP HERE, MY CONTACTS WILL WELD THEMSELVES TO MY EYEBALLS.

I'LL TAKE THEM OUT AND HOLD THEM IN MY HANDS!! YES!! I'LL SLEEP SITTING STRAIGHT UP IN MY CHAIR WITH ONE CONTACT CLUTCHED IN EACH HAND AND I WON'T MOVE UNTIL MORNING!!

IN THE LAST MOMENTS OF CONSCIOUSNESS, THE HUMAN SPIRIT RALLIES PAST WHAT IS MERELY DIFFICULT AND EMBRACES THE IMPOSSIBLE.

WHILE YOU WERE OUT, CATHY, YOUR YOUNG SWEETIE CALLED AND ASKED YOU OUT FOR A ROMANTIC DINNER.

WHILE YOU WERE OUT, ANDREA, **YOUR** YOUNG SWEETIE GOT HERSELF EXPELLED FROM DAY CAMP, COMPUTER CLASS AND THE KICKBALL TEAM, AND IS NOW AT HOME WITH YOUR HUSBAND WHERE SHE APPARENTLY SPENT HER "TIME OUT" TEACHING NAUGHTY WORDS TO YOUR EVEN YOUNGER SWEETIE.

I DON'T WANT TO TRADE PLACES...BUT, JUST ONCE, I WISH I COULD TRADE MESSAGES.

THANKS FOR COMING WITH ME, CATHY. THE BACK-TO-SCHOOL SHOPPING SCENE IS SO WILD.

EVERYWHERE YOU LOOK, KIDS ARE RUNNING, SHRIEKING, WHINING, BEGGING, FIGHTING, THROWING THINGS...

OUCH!
OOCH!
MINE!

WHAT'S WRONG WITH YOU PEOPLE?? CAN'T YOU CONTROL YOUR CHILDREN??!

THOSE ARE YOUR CHILDREN, ANDREA.

WAAH!

HOW MANY TIMES DOES A WOMAN RELIVE THE EMOTION OF BECOMING A MOTHER?....

BONK!
SPLAT!
RIP!

ZENITH: BORN AT THE PEAK OF OVER-ACHIEVER YUPPIEDOM. READ TO IN UTERO. FLASH CARDS FROM DAY ONE. ALL GENDER-SPECIFIC, NON-EDUCATIONAL TOYS BANNED FROM HOME. OBSESSIVE SENSORY STIMULATION FROM ONE CONSTANT, ATTENTIVE PARENT.

GUS: BORN DURING THE "RETURN TO FAMILY VALUES" ECONOMIC SLUMP. TEETHED ON THE REMOTE CONTROL. IN AND OUT OF VARIOUS CHEAP DAY-CARE CENTERS. SLEEPS WITH A PLASTIC RIFLE ON POWER RANGER SHEETS.

TWO UNIQUE LITTLE SOULS. TWO ENTIRELY DIFFERENT UPBRINGINGS. BONDED FOREVER BY A FORCE MORE POWERFUL THAN ALL OTHER INPUT COMBINED...

GAP KIDS! GAP KIDS! GAP KIDS!

PEER PRESSURE.

THE MOTHER OF THEM ALL.

THIS WOULD BE A NICE PLAY OUTFIT FOR SCHOOL, ZENITH!

I'M NOT GOING TO PRESCHOOL LOOKING LIKE A DORK, MOM.

SILLY ME. OF COURSE I RESPECT YOUR RIGHT TO MAKE CHOICES. DO YOU LIKE THE DUCK PATTERN OR THE BUMBLEBEE PRINT?

GROSS ME OUT.

I KNOW THAT DISAGREEMENT IS A HEALTHY EXPRESSION OF SEPARATION ANXIETY, BUT...

COOL! DOC MARTENS!

...MOMMY STILL CONTROLS THE MONEY!!

YEAH, RIGHT..

YOUR SON JUST ATE A PAIR OF NIKES. WILL THAT BE CHARGE?

CHLOE HAS $60 JEANS! WHY CAN'T I HAVE $60 JEANS?!

CHLOE'S MOTHER IS A WIMP, ZENITH.

YOUR MOMMY HAS SPENT HER WHOLE LIFE TRYING TO BE AN INTELLIGENT, PRODUCTIVE, POWERFUL ROLE MODEL OF WOMANHOOD, AND SHE IS **NOT** GOING TO CAVE IN TO A FOUR-YEAR-OLD WITH AN ATTITUDE!!

IF YOU WEREN'T AT THE OFFICE ALL DAY, I WOULDN'T BE SO HUNGRY FOR ACCEPTANCE AND SUSCEPTIBLE TO PEER PRESSURE.

THAT WAS REALLY LOW.

DYLAN HAS A CD-ROM. CAN I HAVE A CD-ROM?

YOU LET OUR FOUR-YEAR-OLD TALK YOU INTO DESIGN-ER TENNIS SHOES, ANDREA ??

IT'S OK TO GIVE IN ON THE SMALLER ISSUES AS LONG AS WE STICK TO OUR GUNS ON THE IMPORTANT ONES, HONEY.

DKNY

SO FAR, WE'VE GIVEN IN ON CLOTHING, CANDY, SOFT DRINKS, PLASTIC WEAPONS, BARBIE DOLLS, TV, VIDEO, BATH TIME, BEDTIME, MANNERS, NEAT-NESS AND SHARING.

DKNY

CHOC POPS

ONE OF THESE DAYS, WE'RE REALLY GOING TO GET TOUGH!

KEEP IT DOWN, YOU TWO! WE'RE TRYING TO WATCH "HARD COPY."

ALL ZENITH TALKED ABOUT ALL SUMMER WAS GETTING A "TRINI" POWER RANGERS OUT-FIT LIKE YOUR LITTLE BRIANA HAS!

OH, BRIANA WON'T WEAR THAT ANY-MORE! "TRINI'S" OUT.

ESCHOOL

WHAT DO YOU MEAN, "TRINI'S" OUT ?? ZENITH PLANNED FOR WEEKS TO WEAR HER "TRINI" OUTFIT ON THE FIRST DAY OF SCHOOL!

NO. "TRINI'S" THE YELLOW ONE. THIS YEAR ALL THE GIRLS ARE DRESS-ING LIKE "KIMBERLY," THE PINK ONE!

PRESCHOOL

MY BABY'S IN THERE IN HER PROUD LITTLE YELLOW "TRINI" OUTFIT... AND ALL THE OTHER GIRLS HAVE DESERTED HER FOR THE "KIMBERLY" GET-UP?!

PRESCHOOL

SHOULD HAVE KEPT UP WITH THE PLAY-DATES THIS SUMMER, HUH ?

AAGH!

GUILT, 101: WE RE-ENROLL EVERY YEAR.

ESCH

ANDREA'S KIDS WON'T WEAR ANYTHING THAT DOESN'T HAVE A BRAND NAME OR LICENSED CHARACTER ON IT, MOM.

UM, HM!

WHAT'S THAT SUPPOSED TO MEAN?

I JUST SAID, "UM, HM".

YOUR "UM, HM!" HAD THAT "AH, HAH!" TONE, AS THOUGH YOU WERE ACCUSING HER OF BECOMING A CLICHÉ OF THE OVERLY PERMISSIVE, GUILT-RIDDEN WORKING MOTHER ...AND I DON'T WANT TO HEAR ABOUT IT, MOM!

UM, HM!

AACK! I DON'T WANT TO HEAR THAT SPEECH, EITHER!

EVERY YEAR I GET MORE ELOQUENT WITH FEWER WORDS.

94

96

NOTHING EXEMPLIFIES THIS SEASON'S REFINED ELEGANCE LIKE THE GRACEFUL, TASTEFUL, CLASSIC MID-KNEE SKIRT.

OF COURSE, IT LOOKS A LITTLE FRUMPY ON ITS OWN, SO YOU'LL WANT TO SAUCE IT UP WITH NAKED, SEAMED HOSE, TARTY STILETTO HEELS, A VAMPY FUCHSIA BOA AND A SMEAR OF BLAZING SCARLET LIPSTICK!

WHAT HAPPENED TO REFINED ELEGANCE?

OH, IT'S A FEELING YOU CARRY ON THE INSIDE...

...IN YOUR PADDED, PUSH-UP "WONDER BRA"!

OUT WITH LAST YEAR'S JUVENILE FRILLS AND TODDLER FLATS...IN WITH THIS YEAR'S CHISELED WAIST AND SKYSCRAPER HEELS!

OUT WITH LAST YEAR'S FLIMSY, FORLORN FABRICS... ...IN WITH THIS YEAR'S HIGH-VOLTAGE VINYLS AND DAY-GLO RUBBER JACKETS!

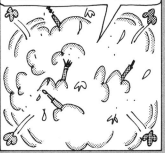

OUT WITH LAST YEAR'S BARE-FACED WAIFS... IN WITH THIS YEAR'S SCREAMING CRIMSON LIPS, VIOLET EYESHADOW AND GOLDEN UP-SWEPT HAIR!!

GOODBYE, BABY DOLL. HELLO, BARBIE DOLL.

GUESS WHO BURNED MORE CALORIES DURING LUNCH HOUR?

CHARLENE: DID A SIX-MILE POWER WALK WHILE SUCKING ON AN ICE CUBE MADE FROM FROZEN MINERAL WATER.

KIM: RAN 20 MINUTES ON THE TREADMILL FOLLOWED BY A 40-MINUTE STEP CLASS.

CATHY: DROVE TO THE MALL. TRIED ON A RED RUBBER DRESS.

YES! PERFECT! THIS IS WHAT FALL FASHION IS ALL ABOUT!!

SAVAGE GRACE! BRAZEN BEAUTY! FIERCELY CHIC! DANGEROUS SEXINESS! A STRONG, HEADY, HIGH-POWERED FEMININITY!!

GEEZ...WHAT HAPPENED TO YOU??

BONK!

THE SOPHISTICAT-ED, STREAM-LINED, KNEE-LENGTH SUIT.

TOO OLD.

THE SASSY KILT WITH SHRUNK-EN MOHAIR SWEATER!

TOO YOUNG.

OR, FOR THOSE WHO FALL RIGHT IN BETWEEN, THE SHRUNKEN TOP WITH KNEE-LENGTH SKIRT!

NO! THE IN-BETWEEN ZONE?! I'M IN THE DREADED IN-BETWEEN ZONE??!

THE MID-LIFE CRISIS: THIS FALL'S GIFT WITH PURCHASE.

I'VE WORN NOTHING BUT MUTED BEIGE TONES FOR TWO YEARS. I CAN'T WEAR A BRIGHT RED DRESS.

OF COURSE YOU CAN! THIS SEASON IS ALL ABOUT COLOR!

ELECTRIC RED! SCREAMING TANGERINE! RETINA-SEARING FUCHSIA! BOLD, AGGRESSIVE, "ISN'T IT A BLAST TO BE A WOMAN?!" COLOR!!!!

THANK YOU. NOW I'M GOING TO DRIVE MY TAN CAR TO MY OFF-WHITE HOME, PUT ON MY EGGSHELL BATHROBE, CURL UP ON MY ECRU FURNITURE, EAT A BUNCH OF OATMEAL COOKIES, AND PRETEND WE NEV-ER HAD THIS CONVERSATION.

ANOTHER CUSTOMER LOCKED IN HER IVORY TOWER.

BLACK IS OUT TOO UNLESS IT'S SHINY AND VINYL!!

YOU'RE GETTING SLEEPY... VERY, VERY SLEEPY...

YOUR EYELIDS ARE GETTING HEAVY... THE REST OF YOU FEELS LIKE CEMENT...

YOU WILL SIT AND FREE YOUR MIND...YES...FREE OF INHIBITIONS...FREE OF BUDGET WORRIES...FREE OF COMMON SENSE...COMPLETELY FREE...

BOOTNOTIZED.

WHEN SHE COMES TO, SHE WON'T REMEMBER ANYTHING AT ALL.

HOW ARE THE STILETTO PUMPS?

THEY CRUSH MY TOES, CRIPPLE MY ANKLES, AND WAD MY CALF MUSCLES UP INTO LITTLE KNOTS.

THEY LOOK DESPERATE AND CHEAP AND INSULT THE SELF-WORTH OF ALL WOMEN BY MAKING IT IMPOSSIBLE TO EVEN WALK WITHOUT ASSISTANCE!

THEY TAKE TWO INCHES OFF THE PERCEIVED WIDTH OF YOUR THIGHS.

SOLD!

RETAIL GETS BACK TO BASICS.

WHAT HAPPENED TO THE "FRESH, DEWY FACE"?

IT TURNS OUT THE ONLY "DEWY" PART WAS WOMEN WEEPING WHEN THEY GOT A LOOK AT THEMSELVES IN BROAD DAYLIGHT WITH NO MAKEUP.

WHAT HAPPENED TO "REVELING IN THE FACES OUR FABULOUS, INTERESTING LIVES HAVE EARNED"?

ONE TOO MANY AGING SUPERMODEL WAS CAUGHT SNEAKING INTO THE LADIES' ROOM WITH A TUBE OF "ERASE."

WHAT HAPPENED TO THE "WHOLESOME, HEALTHY INNOCENCE OF EARTH TONES"?

FRUMPY, DUMPY, GRUMPY AND BOR-ING.

OH, MISS..?

PLEASE! I CAN ONLY MAKE OVER ONE BRAIN AT A TIME!!

99

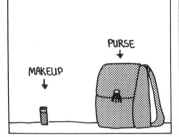

WORKING

DOUBLE CLICK THE ICON TO OPEN THE FOLDER...NO. CLICK **ONCE** TO OPEN THE **FILE**, **THEN** CLICK TO OPEN THE FOLDER... NO. SCROLL TO THE HELP MENU...

COOKING

THE FOUR-MINUTE TURKEY TETRAZZINI... NO. THE SIX-MINUTE VEGETABLE LASAGNA.. ...NO. THE TWO MINUTE CHICK-EN ENCHILADA ....

BANKING

SECRET CODE #4237...
...NO. #4238...
...NO. #4328...
...NO. #3248...
...NO. #2348...

TIME SPENT SEEKING INSTANT GRATIFICATION TODAY: 4½ HOURS.

I WORKED FOR A MONTH TO GET MY OFFICE UNDER CONTROL. TURNED MY BACK FOR AN HOUR... EVERYTHING WAS CHAOS.

I WORKED FOR A WEEK TO GET MY OFFICE UNDER CONTROL. TURNED MY BACK FOR TEN MINUTES...EVERYTHING WAS CHAOS.

I WORKED ALL DAY TO GET MY OFFICE UNDER CONTROL. TURNED MY BACK FOR TWO SECONDS...EVERYTHING WAS CHAOS.

I DON'T NEED MORE SPACE. I NEED A SECURITY GUARD.

ATTENTION ALL EMPLOYEES: THE COMPANY OF THE FUTURE IS A HAPPY, HEALTHY, STRESS-FREE TEAM!

THUS, I'M PLEASED TO ANNOUNCE OUR NEW POLICY OF ENCOURAGING ALL WORKERS TO LEAVE AT 5:00, TAKE A FULL LUNCH HOUR AND NEVER WORK ON WEEKENDS!

COMBINED WITH OUR **OTHER** NEW POLICY OF DOWN-SIZING, THIS MEANS YOU'LL BE EXPEC-TED TO CHEERFULLY DO TWICE THE WORK IN HALF THE TIME!

THE THANKS I GET FOR BEING AN EVOLVED BOSS...

GOOD MORNING, STAFF! WE'LL BEGIN TODAY WITH A LIGHT STRETCH 'N' STEP CLASS TO ELEVATE CORPORATE SPIRIT AND LOWER CORPORATE HEALTH INSURANCE CLAIMS.

STRETCH 'N' STEP

AT 10:00, WE'LL HAVE A CLEANSING CARROT JUICE BREAK, FOLLOWED BY AN INSPIRATIONAL READING FROM "THE STRESS-FREE OFFICE" AND A DEMONSTRATION OF WORK STATION RELAXATION TECHNIQUES.

REFRESH 'N' REFLECT

WE'LL ADJOURN FOR A FAT-FREE VEGGIE LUNCH, AND THEN SPEND THE AFTERNOON DISCUSSING WAYS TO USE OUR TIME MORE EFFECTIVELY SO WE CAN GO HOME AT 5:00, RELAXED AND READY TO ENJOY AN EVENING OF REAL QUALITY TIME WITH LOVED ONES.

OUT OF MY WAY, ELECTRA! I HAVE WORK TO DO!!

RATS. SHE HAD ANOTHER GOOD DAY AT THE OFFICE.

IN IN

YOU DON'T WANT ME TO WORK LATE ANYMORE!

CORRECT! IT'S UNHEALTHFUL AND PASSÉ!

I DON'T WANT TO WORK LATE ANYMORE!

CORRECT! YOU DESERVE A LIFE!

HOWEVER, IF I DON'T WORK LATE, THIS WON'T GET DONE, WE'LL LOSE THE ACCOUNT, GO OUT OF BUSINESS, AND I WON'T BE WORKING AT ALL.

CORRECT AGAIN!

I THINK I'LL WORK LATE.

SOME PEOPLE JUST CAN'T LEARN TO LET GO.

I COULD IMPROVE THE QUALITY OF MY LIFE BY CUTTING MY HOURS AND SPENDING MORE TIME WITH MY KIDS!

SAVINGS TO ME: $15.50 PER HOUR.

I COULD IMPROVE THE QUALITY OF MY LIFE BY TAKING A MONTH LEAVE OF ABSENCE TO DO MEANINGFUL CHARITY WORK!

SAVINGS TO ME: $3,300.00.

I COULD IMPROVE THE QUALITY OF MY LIFE BY SAYING NO TO A PROMOTION AND THE STRESS THAT COMES WITH IT!

SAVINGS TO ME: $4,500.00.

I COULD IMPROVE THE QUALITY OF MY LIFE BY GETTING A GIANT RAISE!

HONESTLY... SOME PEOPLE AND THEIR WARPED VALUES...

105

WHAT DO YOU THINK OF A GROWN PERSON MOVING BACK HOME WITH HIS OR HER PARENTS, MOM?

IT'S THE ULTIMATE STATEMENT OF MATURITY AND SELF-CONFIDENCE, CATHY! AN UNPARALLELED EXPRESSION OF WHOLESOME VALUES!

YES, SWEETIE! COME HOME! COME HOME AND LET US BE A REAL FAMILY AGAIN!!

NOT ME, MOM. MY BOYFRIEND IS MOVING HOME WITH HIS MOTHER.

WELL, THAT'S JUST PATHETIC.

WELL, THAT'S IT! I'M PACKED AND READY TO MOVE!

WHERE ARE THE REST OF YOUR CLOTHES?

I DON'T HAVE ANY.

WHERE ARE YOUR DISHES?

I DON'T HAVE ANY.

WHERE'S YOUR FURNITURE?

I DON'T HAVE ANY.

WHERE'S YOUR STUFF?? THE NORMAL HUMAN STUFF OF LIFE??

I DON'T REALLY HAVE ANY.

THE CLASSIC DILEMMA: DO I BREAK UP NOW, OR DO I STAY WITH HIM BECAUSE I HAVE IDEAS FOR THE NEXT 40 GIFT-GIVING OCCASIONS?

I HAVE A LIFE-SAPPING MORTGAGE. YOU'RE MOVING HOME WITH YOUR MOM TO SAVE #300 ON RENT...

I'M TRYING TO SCRAPE TOGETHER MONEY FOR A RETIREMENT ACCOUNT. YOU'RE SAVING UP FOR A NEW BIKE... I HAVE A HOME FULL OF FURNITURE ON MY CHARGE CARDS. YOU OWN ONE BOX OF CD'S!

WE HAVE NOTHING IN COMMON, ALEX! NOTHING AT ALL!!

SURE WE DO! WE'RE BOTH BROKE!

I HAVE MORE TO NOT SHOW FOR IT!

I WANTED TO PROVE I COULD EAT ONE PIECE OF HALLOWEEN CANDY AND STOP. THAT WAS MY MISSION AND MY GOAL!

AND I **DID** IT! I ATE THE CANDY, DRANK EIGHT GLASSES OF WATER AND SPENT THE REST OF THE EVENING IN THE BATHROOM...BUT I **DID** IT! I ATE ONE PIECE OF CANDY AND STOPPED!

I SPENT THE EVENING PLAYING FRENCH LANGUAGE TAPES FOR MY UNBORN SON WHILE I PRE-LABELED ALL MY CHRISTMAS CARD ENVELOPES.

I WIN!!

MONDAY: DAY ONE OF DIET. LED A FULL, PRODUCTIVE, ACTIVE LIFE.

WEDNESDAY: DAY THREE OF DIET. ACCOMPLISHED SOME THINGS. DEVOTED REST OF DAY TO LOW-FAT MEAL PLANNING.

FRIDAY: DAY FIVE OF DIET. SAT IN MOTIONLESS STUPOR WAITING FOR NEXT ALLOWABLE FOOD PORTION.

I HAVEN'T LOST ANY WEIGHT, BUT MY BRAIN HAS SHRUNK TWO SIZES.

POUNDS DON'T MATTER. ALL THAT COUNTS IS A COMMITMENT TO POSITIVE FOOD CHOICES...

...A NUTRITION/EXERCISE PROGRAM THAT MAXIMIZES HEALTH AND ALLOWS THE BODY TO HONOR ITS OWN NATURAL WEIGHT.

:CLICK:

I'M NOT DIETING. I'M DOWNSIZING.

SHALL I DRESS UP AS THE NO-NONSENSE OVERACHIEVER IN A POWER SUIT...

...OR SHOULD I BE THE NURTURING EARTH MOTHER IN FLOWING SKIRT AND TUNIC...

...NO. I'LL BE THE SAUCY WORKING GAL WHO HASN'T LOST TOUCH OF HER FEMININITY...

...NO. I'LL BE THE WATER-BOTTLE-TOTING URBAN COWGIRL...NO...

FOR SOME OF US, EVERY DAY IS HALLOWEEN.

I BROUGHT THE LEFTOVER CUPCAKES FROM MY SON'S HALLOWEEN PARTY SO HE WOULDN'T EAT ANY MORE OF THEM.

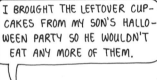

I HAD TO GET ALL OUR LEFTOVER HALLOWEEN CANDY OUT OF THE HOUSE!

I DON'T WANT MY KIDS EATING THIS JUNK, AND I DON'T WANT TO EAT IT!

JUST LEAVE IT IN THE COFFEE ROOM! SOMEONE ELSE WILL EAT IT!

ANOTHER UNSUSPECTING VICTIM HEADS TOWARD A 4,500-CALORIE CUP OF COFFEE.

HOW COULD I GAIN WEIGHT?? I'VE BEEN DATING A FITNESS TRAINER FOR TEN MONTHS!

ALL WE EVER DO IS EXERCISE! ALL WE EVER TALK ABOUT IS NUTRITION AND MUSCLE GROUPS! EVERY FREE MOMENT IS DEVOTED TO HEALTH!

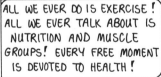

WHEN DID YOU FIND TIME TO GAIN WEIGHT?? WHEN?? WHEN?? WHEN??

...THE FINAL HOLDOVER FROM THE '80s: OVERACHIEVER FAT CELLS.

112

Panel 1: FOIL-WRAPPED CHOCOLATE SANTAS! THESE WOULD BE PERFECT TO PUT IN MOM'S STOCKING THIS YEAR!

PRE-CHRISTMAS SAL
SANTAS SANTAS SANTAS

Panel 2: ...BUT I SHOULD SAMPLE ONE TO MAKE SURE THEY'RE JUST LIKE THE ONES MOM USED TO BUY FOR ME...

Shop Early Fo

Panel 3: ...NO. BETTER TO SAMPLE TWO. ONE IS A TEST. TWO IS A REAL SAMPLE.....NO. FOUR RANDOM SANTAS MUST BE EATEN TO ASSURE CONSISTENT QUALITY THROUGHOUT THE BOX...

Panel 4: THE SHOPPING HASN'T STARTED, BUT I'M EIGHT WEEKS AHEAD ON MY HOLIDAY EATING.

Panel 5: I HAVEN'T DONE MY WORKOUT IN A MONTH, ALEX.

LOTS OF PEOPLE GET OFF TRACK, CATHY.

Panel 6: I HAVEN'T WORKED OUT, AND I'VE COMPLETELY BLOWN MY FOOD PROGRAM!

PERFECTLY NORMAL. EVERYONE HAS SETBACKS.

STAFF

Panel 7: I HAVEN'T WORKED OUT, HAVE BLOWN MY FOOD PROGRAM, HAVE REVERTED BACK TO EVERY BAD EATING HABIT, AND HAVE BEEN LYING AROUND LIKE A HOPELESS BLOB!!

Panel 8: WELCOME TO THE CLUB! WE'VE ALL BEEN THERE!

IS THERE NO AREA LEFT IN WHICH I CAN PAVE THE WAY?

STAFF

Panel 9: I GOT UP TWO HOURS EARLY, ORGANIZED MY OFFICE, AND FOR ONCE HAVE TIME TO FLIP AHEAD IN MY CALENDAR AND MAKE SOME PLANS...

Panel 10: HI, ALEX. I'M INVITING YOU AND YOUR MOM FOR THANKSGIVING! LET'S INTRODUCE THE WOMAN WHO HATES ME TO THE PARENTS WHO ADORE ME WHILE EATING THE FIRST FULL MEAL I'VE EVER COOKED IN MY LIFE! WHY NOT? HA, HA! I CAN HANDLE ANYTHING!!

Panel 11: (no text)

Panel 12: THE EARLY BIRD GETS THE CAN OF WORMS.

113

WILL YOU COME FOR THANKSGIVING DINNER THIS YEAR, CHARLENE?

OH, GREAT. THE BUFFER GUEST.

WHAT?

YOU'RE NERVOUS ABOUT YOUR PARENTS MEETING ALEX'S MOTHER, AND WANT ME THERE AS THE BUFFER GUEST.

I'M **NOT** ASKING YOU TO BE THE BUFFER GUEST, CHARLENE! I'M INVITING YOU AND YOUR HUSBAND TO SHARE A SPECIAL HOLIDAY MEAL WITH MY LOVED ONES!

OH, GREAT. THE BUFFER COUPLE.

CAN I PUT YOU DOWN TO BRING THE CONVERSATION?

THANKSGIVING DINNER IS AT MY HOUSE THIS YEAR, MOM!

DON'T BE SILLY, SWEETIE. YOU CAN'T DO IT ALL BY YOURSELF!

WHY NOT? I ONLY INVITED SIX PEOPLE.

OH, HEAVENS! I'LL COME RIGHT OVER AND HELP YOU MAKE A SCHEDULE!

MOM, THANKSGIVING ISN'T FOR TWO WEEKS! BELIEVE ME, I'M USED TO DEADLINES! I'LL SIMPLY RUN TO THE STORE THE NIGHT BEFORE, BUY SOME GROCERIES, POP THEM IN THE OVEN, SET THE TABLE, AND VOILÁ! WHAT'S ALL THE FUSS?

CATHY WILL BE COOKING HER OWN GOOSE THIS YEAR, DEAR.

YOU DIDN'T HAVE TO BUY NEW PLACEMATS JUST BECAUSE MY MOM'S COMING FOR THANKSGIVING, CATHY.

I NEEDED SOME ANYWAY, ALEX.

...UH, OH. THE NEW PLACEMATS MAKE MY TABLE LOOK OUTDATED...THEY MAKE THE WALLS LOOK KIND OF GRUNGY...

COMPARED TO THE NEW PLACEMATS, IT **ALL** LOOKS WRONG! I HAVE TO GET RID OF THAT OLD SOFA! I HAVE TO GET RID OF THAT ICKY LAMP AND HORRID RUG! I....

WHY DON'T YOU JUST GET RID OF THE NEW PLACEMATS?

MEN ARE ALWAYS SO BLIND TO THE OBVIOUS SOLUTION.

HELLO, AND WELCOME TO THE HOME FURNISHINGS REVOLUTION! AN ENTIRE NEW NICHE OF HIP, HAPPENING FURNITURE AIMED AT THE NESTING BABY BOOMER!

YOU WANT AN ARTY, ECLECTIC LIVING SPACE, BUT YOU DON'T HAVE THE MONEY OR TASTE... YOU WANT TO MAKE A STATEMENT, BUT YOU WANT TO MAKE IT BY 7:00PM...

...AND AS THE HOLIDAYS DRAW NEAR, THE URGE IS TO BUY ALL NEW FURNITURE AND ENTERTAIN AT HOME RATHER THAN GO TO OTHER PEOPLE'S HOMES AND HAVE TO FIGURE OUT WHAT TO WEAR!

I'M NOT JUST THE TARGET MARKET. I HAVE A BULLSEYE PAINTED ON MY WALLET.

MY WHOLE HOUSE IS WRONG, CHARLENE! LOOK... I NEED A HIP LIVING ROOM ENSEMBLE LIKE THIS...

I NEED SLOUCHY FABRICS... TRENDY ART BOOKS...BASKETS OF AVANT-GARDE MAGAZINES ...POTS ON THE FLOOR... ETCHINGS ON THE WALLS... FOLK ART FIGURINES... ETHNIC THROW RUGS...AND..AND...

OH, FOR CRYING OUT LOUD, CATHY! WHO ARE YOU TRYING TO IMPRESS??

MAY I HELP YOU?

YES. IF I BUY "GROUPING B," DOES IT COME WITH SOME WITTY, WITH-IT FRIENDS?

I BOUGHT NEW PLACEMATS, AND SUDDENLY I'M REDECORATING MY WHOLE HOUSE TO GO WITH THEM.

THAT'S NOTHING! I BOUGHT A NEW ROLL OF PAPER TOWELS ONCE AND WAS COMPELLED TO REMODEL MY KITCHEN!

I BOUGHT A PRETTY NEW BAR OF SOAP ONCE AND WOUND UP GUTTING THE BATHROOM, REDOING THE BEDROOM, AND INSTALLING HARDWOOD FLOORS!

THERE ARE NO SMALL PURCHASES, ONLY SMALL IMAGINATIONS.

I'D WRITE THAT DOWN, BUT I'M AFRAID OF WHAT WOULD HAPPEN IF I BOUGHT A NEW PENCIL.

THIS ONE. ...NO. THIS ONE. ...NO.

YOU'VE SPENT LONGER DECIDING ON A $150 TABLE THAN ON A $200 PAIR OF BOOTS, CATHY.

A BOOT BLUNDER CAN BE SHOVED UNDER THE BED, CHARLENE. A BAD DRESS CAN BE STUFFED IN THE CLOSET...

...AND ANY AND ALL ERRORS IN JUDGMENT ON LINGERIE, BEAUTY PRODUCTS AND SMALL APPLIANCES CAN BE STASHED IN THE TRUNK OF MY CAR!

I'M ONLY GOOD AT COMMITTING TO THAT WHICH I CAN HIDE.

WE HAVE SOME FABULOUS ANTIQUE PIECES...

OH, NO. I CAN'T AFFORD GENUINELY OLD FURNITURE.

I WANT NEW FURNITURE THAT LOOKS OLD.

AH, YES... WE HAVE THE CHIPPED PAINT LOOK... THE CRACKLED PAINT LOOK...

...THE FADED, PEELING PAINT LOOK... OR, FOR A LITTLE EXTRA, THE GOUGED WOOD UNDER THE CHIPPED, CRACKLED, FADED AND PEELING PAINT LOOK!

WHAT'S WRONG WITH THE FURNITURE YOU ALREADY HAVE?

IT'S TOO OLD.

DISASSEMBLED DINING ROOM TABLE STRAPPED TO THE ROOF... DINING ROOM CHAIRS JAMMED IN THE BACKSEAT...

...FLATTENED BOOKCASE STICKING OUT OF THE TRUNK... UNCONSTRUCTED END TABLES, LAMPS, POTS, RUGS AND CURTAIN RODS IN THE FRONT SEAT...

I CAN'T GET IT ALL IN. YOU SHOULD HAVE BROUGHT YOUR MINIVAN.

OH, PLEASE. I HARDLY THINK I FIT THE DO-IT-YOURSELFER MINIVAN CLICHÉ!

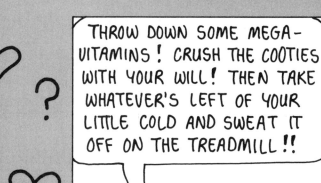

117

SHOULD I LEAVE ALEX'S PICTURE OUT WHEN HIS MOTHER COMES FOR THANKSGIVING, OR HIDE IT IN A DRAWER?

...DISPLAY THE PICTURE IN THE BEDROOM, OR PUT IT IN THE LIVING ROOM?... MIX IT IN WITH "GENERAL FRIEND" PICTURES, OR GIVE IT A "SPECIAL FRIEND" SPOT?... PUT IT HERE? ...OR HIDE IT HERE?...OR... WHAT AM I DOING??

I STILL HAVE TO PAINT TWO ROOMS, ASSEMBLE A COFFEE TABLE, PLAN THE MEAL, BUY GROCERIES, CLEAN THE HOUSE AND COOK A FEAST FOR SEVEN! **WHAT AM I DOING WANDERING AROUND WITH A SNAPSHOT OF MY BOYFRIEND??!**

I MAY NOT SEE THE BIG PICTURE, BUT I NEVER LOSE SIGHT OF A 4x6.

TO DO BY THU

HELLO?

AACK! QUICK, MOM! IF THE RECIPE SAYS A CUP OF ONIONS, IS THAT BEFORE OR AFTER THEY'RE CHOPPED??

IF I FORGOT TO BUY BASIL, WILL ANY GREEN FLAKEY THING IN A SMALL JAR DO? WERE THE SWEET POTATOES SUPPOSED TO BE PEELED BEFORE I MASHED THEM? HOW AM I SUPPOSED TO MAKE GRAVY FROM THE DRIPPINGS IF MY TURKEY ISN'T DRIPPING? CAN CROUTONS BE CHOPPED-UP TOAST?

I'LL BE HAPPY TO COME OVER AND HELP, CATHY.

HELP? NO! I DON'T NEED HELP!

A MOTHER'S PLACE IS IN THE KITCHEN...SITTING BY THE PHONE, WAITING FOR HER DAUGHTER TO CALL FROM **HER** KITCHEN.

WHAT WAS I THINKING, INVITING ALL OF YOU FOR THANKSGIVING?? I TRIED TO REDECORATE IN TWO DAYS! I TRIED TO LEARN TO COOK IN ONE NIGHT!!

I'VE BEEN UP SINCE 5:00 AM, AND NOTHING'S READY! MY HAIR IS MATTED WITH PIE MIX! I'M WEARING THE SWEATSUIT I SLEPT IN! THE HOUSE IS A COMPLETE DISASTER!

AND NOW I'M WEEPING IN FRONT OF THE PEOPLE I MOST WANTED TO IMPRESS! **WHAT AM I DOING?? WHAT WAS I THINKING?? WHY?? WHY??**

IT'S A HOLIDAY TRADITION HANDED DOWN FROM GRANDMA: STIR UP THE PITY, AND NO ONE WILL NOTICE THE LUMPS IN THE GRAVY.

THE THANKSGIVING PARTY:

* ONE FIRST-TIME HOSTESS
* ONE YOUNG BOYFRIEND OF HOSTESS, WHO LIVES WITH MOTHER
* ONE MOTHER OF BOYFRIEND, ALMOST SAME AGE AS HOSTESS
* ONE EX-BOYFRIEND OF HOSTESS
* ONE BEST FRIEND OF HOSTESS, BRIDE OF EX-BOYFRIEND OF HOSTESS
* ONE SET OF MORTIFIED PARENTS OF HOSTESS

A ROOM SO FILLED WITH ANXIETY, TENSION, JEALOUSY, AGGRAVATION, HOSTILITY AND NERVES, IT'S HARD TO FATHOM HOW EXPLOSIVE THE CONVERSATION WILL BE...

THE THANKSGIVING CONVERSATION:

OH, LOOK WHAT A CUTE THING YOUR DOG JUST DID!

THANKSGIVING DINNER WAS OVER IN TWENTY MINUTES.

I AGONIZED FOR WEEKS... I PREPARED FOR DAYS... AND THE WHOLE MEAL WAS OVER IN TWENTY MINUTES!

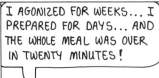

HOW COULD SOMETHING THAT TOOK THAT MUCH WORK ONLY LAST FOR TWENTY MINUTES?!!

OF COURSE, TECHNICALLY, WE'RE ALL STILL EATING, SWEETIE.

DOESN'T COUNT. THE FOOD'S COLD, AND WE'RE STANDING UP.

MY THANKSGIVING DINNER WAS GREAT, WASN'T IT, CHARLENE?

THE TURKEY WAS BURNED, AND THE SWEET POTATOES HAD GLOBS OF PEEL IN THEM.

EVERYONE RAVED! I CAN'T WAIT TO ENTERTAIN AGAIN!

THE CLAMMY SILENCE THAT FILLED THE ROOM WAS MATCHED ONLY BY THE TEMPERATURE AND TEXTURE OF YOUR BEAN DISH.

OH, HA, HA! WHAT A KIDDER! EVERYONE SAID THEY HAD A FABULOUS TIME!

I'LL HELP YOU WITH **YOUR** NEXT DINNER PARTY!

FROM THE MERCY OF POLITE DINNER GUESTS, ANOTHER CATERER IS BORN...

FURNITURE CATALOGS FROM FIVE STORES...UNASSEMBLED PARTS FOR THREE TABLES...

TWENTY-NINE PAINT CHIPS... NINETY-SIX FABRIC SWATCHES... FOUR PARTLY DONE WINDOW TREATMENTS...ONE BAG OF WALL-PAPER...AND TEN MAGAZINES FILLED WITH FABULOUS IDEAS...

ANOTHER HIP, CREATIVE DECORATING SCHEME IS ABANDONED FOR SOMETHING A BIT MORE CLASSIC...

...THE "I-GOT-USED-TO-IT-IN-THE-HALF-FINISHED-STATE" LOOK.

HO, HUM. NOTHING TO DO TONIGHT. LET'S GO TO BED EARLY.

I'VE UNFOLDED 56 VERSIONS OF THE EXACT SAME SWEATER FOR YOU...

I'VE CALLED EVERY BRANCH OF OUR STORE TO SEE IF IT EXISTS IN A SLIGHTLY PINKER MAUVE... I'VE LOST 10 OTHER CUSTOMERS WHILE YOU FORCED ME INTO A DISCUSSION OF WEAVE IRREGULARITIES....

YOU NOW HAVE FIVE SECONDS TO MAKE A DECISION BEFORE I BLOW! FIVE...FOUR...THREE ...TWO...ONE..

I'LL TAKE IT.

SAY WHAT THEY WILL ABOUT CATALOG SHOPPING, NOTHING WILL EVER REPLACE GOOD OLD EYEBALL-TO-EYEBALL CONTACT.

WHEN YOU'RE LITTLE, 80% OF ALL THE TOYS ARE FOR BOYS, WITH ONE PUNY ROW OF DOLLS FOR GIRLS...

FOR THE REST OF YOUR LIFE, 90% OF THE WHOLE CITY IS GIFTS FOR WOMEN, WITH ONE PUNY ROW OF NECKTIES FOR MEN.

WHAT HAPPENED? HOW DID WE LOSE OUR EDGE??

WHILE YOU BOYS WERE BUSY PLAYING WITH YOUR ACTION FIGURES, THE GIRLS WERE PLOTTING HOW TO TAKE OVER THE MALLS.

"1500 MUSEUM ART POSTERS"... ...I SHOULD SEE THESE... "900 UNIQUE PET GIFTS"... ...WAIT. I HAVE TO GET THIS..

"2000 CLASSIC MOVIES"... "1000 STYLES OF LACE"... "550 GRECIAN REPLICAS"...

YES! SEND ME "52 PAGES OF MINIATURES"! "97 PAGES OF COOKWARE"! "300 PAGES OF COFFEE BEANS"! "200 PAGES OF CRAFT IDEAS"! "500 PAGES OF FREEBIES"!!

HOW'S IT GOING, CATHY?

18 DAYS UNTIL CHRISTMAS, AND THE ONLY THING I'VE ORDERED IS MORE CATALOGS.

WE USED TO RACE ALL OVER TOWN AT THE LAST MINUTE... ...AND NOW LOOK AT US! A HUNDRED DIFFERENT CATALOGS FILLED WITH THOUSANDS OF PERFECT GIFTS!

IMAGINE WHAT GRANDMA WOULD SAY IF SHE KNEW WE COULD GET EVERYTHING WE NEED FOR CHRISTMAS JUST BY PICKING UP THE PHONE!

GRANDMA WOULD SAY, "BETTER NOT ORDER ANYTHING YET! THERE MIGHT BE SOME- THING BETTER IN THE CATALOG THAT MIGHT COME TOMORROW!"

SOME PEOPLE PROCRASTINATE. WE HONOR OUR GENE POOL.

HOW MUCH MORE WILL YOU BE SLASHING THE PRICE ON THIS BLOUSE BEFORE CHRISTMAS?

60% OFF

HOW DESPERATE ARE YOU TO BAIL OUT OF YOUR "SPECIAL BUY" HANDBAG BLUNDER??

SPECIAL BUY 50% OFF

HOW MANY MORE MARKDOWNS BEFORE YOU HIT YOUR COSTUME JEWELRY CRACKING POINT??

40% 60% 80% OFF

GET OUT OF MY STORE!! GET OUT OF MY STORE!!

I HAVEN'T MOVED ANY MERCHANDISE, BUT I'VE UNLOADED ONE CUSTOMER.

40% 60% 80% OFF

SALE

FIRST I'LL GET OUT ALL THE CATALOGS AND MARK ALL THE GIFTS I MIGHT WANT WITH LITTLE YELLOW STICKERS... THEN I'LL HAVE TO SPREAD THE MARKED PAGES OUT IN FRONT OF ME...

EXCEPT I CAN'T SPREAD THEM OUT BECAUSE SOMETIMES THERE ARE THINGS ON BOTH SIDES OF THE SAME PAGE...ALSO, IF I TEAR THE PAGES OUT OF THE CATALOGS, I WON'T KNOW WHICH ONES THEY CAME FROM...

THEN I'LL RUN TO THE COPY SHOP AND COPY THE PAGES I WANT, EXCEPT, OF COURSE, THE BLACK AND WHITE COPIES WON'T DO JUSTICE TO THE ITEMS, SO I'LL HAVE TO GO BACK AND GET COLOR COPIES...THEN I'LL CUT EVERYTHING OUT AND LINE UP SIMILAR ITEMS ON FRESH PAPER, NOTING THE....

THIS IS HOW YOU ORDER FROM A CATA-LOG??

OH, NO. I DON'T ORDER...BUT FOR ONCE, ON DECEMBER 24, I'LL HAVE A BOUND, INDEXED COLLECTION OF EVERYTHING I WISH I'D ORDERED.

40% OFF VELVET JACKETS... I HAVE TO HAVE ONE OF THESE!

60% OFF CASHMERE SWEATERS... I HAVE TO GET ONE OF THESE!

25% OFF PANS... I NEED THESE!

35% OFF BED LINENS... I NEED THESE!

50% OFF TOWELS... I NEED THESE!

I NEED THESE!
I NEED THESE!
I NEED THESE!
I NEED THESE!

HOW'S THE CHRISTMAS SHOPPING GOING, CATHY?

MY SPIRIT OF GIVING DOESN'T KICK IN UNTIL MY SPIRIT OF KEEPING HAS BEEN SATISFIED.

RECEPTIONIST

ALEX WOULD LOVE THIS, BUT I COULDN'T POSSIBLY SPEND THIS MUCH ON HIM....

...THEN AGAIN, HE WON'T KNOW HOW MUCH IT COST...

...BETTER TO SPEND MORE ON ONE PERFECT GIFT THAN TO BUY LOTS OF LITTLE INFERI-OR GIFTS...

....MY TIME IS VALUABLE! IT'S COST-EFFECTIVE FOR ME TO BUY THIS AND BE DONE WITH IT RATHER THAN SPEND THE NEXT WEEK SEARCH-ING FOR SOME-THING CHEAPER...

...HE'S MY BOYFRIEND! A GIFT FOR A BOY-FRIEND IS AN INVEST-MENT IN THE FU-TURE!... NO..WAIT...

MAY I HELP YOU?

WHICH WAY TO THE GIFT RATIONALIZATION DEPARTMENT?

Panel 1: IF YOU SPEND ANOTHER $7 ON MAKEUP FOR YOURSELF, YOU'LL GET THIS BEAUTIFUL GIFT YOU CAN GIVE TO SOMEONE ELSE!

COSMETICS

Panel 2: WHO? ALL MY FRIENDS WILL KNOW I GOT IT FREE BUYING MAKEUP FOR MYSELF!

AH, BUT YOU WEREN'T GOING TO BUY THAT MUCH! YOU SPENT $7 EXTRA ON YOURSELF TO QUALIFY FOR THE FREE GIFT!

COSMETICS

Panel 3: YOU WERE WILLING TO SPRING FOR THE JUMBO ASTRINGENT SO YOUR DEAR FRIEND COULD HAVE A PLASTIC POUCH FULL OF ORANGE LIPSTICKS AND MINI MASCARA WANDS!! A $19.95 VALUE !!!

COSMETICS

Panel 4: ANOTHER SUCCESSFUL MAKEOVER: FROM NARCISSIST TO PHILANTHROPIST.

COSMETICS

GIFT WITH PURCHASE

Panel 5: TO LYNDA...NO. NEEDS AN EXPLANATION FOR WHY I HAVEN'T CALLED....TO JAN.. ..NO. NEEDS AN EXCUSE FOR WHY I HAVEN'T WRITTEN...

envelopes   cards

Panel 6: TO BRENDA...NO. NEEDS A NOTE BEGGING FOR FORGIVENESS FOR FORGETTING HER BIRTHDAY....TO MARCIA...NO. NEEDS A REASON I DIDN'T MAKE IT TO HER PARTY....

envelopes   cards

Panel 7: TO SUE...YES! I JUST MET SUE LAST WEEK! SUE REQUIRES NOTHING! HA,HA! MERRY CHRISTMAS TO SUE !!

envelopes   card

Panel 8: MAKE NEW FRIENDS, BUT KEEP THE OLD. ONE IS SILVER, AND THE OTHERS ALL NEED APOLOGIES.

envelopes   card

Panel 9: HI, CATHY. WHAT'S NEW?

NOTHING'S REALLY HAPPENED SINCE I SAW YOU IN THE MEETING TWENTY MINUTES AGO.

Happy Holidays

Panel 10: HI, CATHY. HOW'S IT GOING?

I SPENT ALL WEEK WORKING ON THE BAKER DEAL WITH YOU. YOU KNOW HOW IT'S GOING.

Happy Holidays

Panel 11: HI, CATHY. HOW ARE YOU DOING?

THE SAME AS I WAS WHEN WE TALKED IN THE ELEVATOR TEN MINUTES AGO. YOU?

PRETTY MUCH THE SAME HERE, TOO.

Panel 12: IF WE HAVE TO HAVE A COMPANY CHRISTMAS PARTY, COULD WE HAVE IT WITH PEOPLE WE HAVEN'T JUST SPENT THE LAST 365 DAYS WITH ?

THE CONFERENCE BOARD SURVEY:

CONSUMER CONFIDENCE IS AT A FOUR-YEAR HIGH, HAVING RISEN TO 101.3 LAST MONTH, UP 12 POINTS SINCE OCTOBER, SIGNALING SOLID GAINS FOR THE HOLIDAY SEASON.

THE APPERT GIFT WRAP INDICATOR:

INCREASED SHIPMENTS OF GIFT WRAP BY MANUFACTURERS INDICATE A POTENTIAL 6.2% REVENUE GAIN FOR THE HOLIDAY SEASON, AN OUTGROWTH OF LOWER UNEMPLOYMENT AND HIGHER CONSUMER SECURITY.

THE DELOITTE AND TOUCHE FORECAST:

77% OF RETAILERS EXPECT HIGHER SALES COMPARED TO 62% WHO EXPECTED INCREASES A YEAR AGO. WIDESPREAD OPTIMISM IS A REFLECTION OF A STRENGTHENED ECONOMY AND POSITIVE, UPBEAT CONSUMER ATTITUDES.

THE HUMAN FACTOR INDEX:

I'M SICK OF BEING FRUGAL! IT'S HOPELESS ANYWAY! WHY NOT JUST BLOW ALL MY MONEY NOW AND WORRY ABOUT IT LATER ?!!

IF I CAN'T DECIDE WHICH GIFTS TO GIVE, IT'S BECAUSE MY MOTHER CAN NEVER DECIDE WHICH GIFTS TO GIVE...

IF I'M BEING TOO MUCH OF A PERFECTIONIST ON MY CHRISTMAS CARDS, IT'S BECAUSE MY FATHER IS TOO MUCH OF A PERFECTIONIST...

I BLAME MY OVERSPENDING ON UNCLE RALPH, MY DISORGANIZATION ON AUNT IRENE, AND ALL CURRENT AND PENDING HOLIDAY WEIGHT GAIN ON THE GRAND LEGACY OF THE FEMALE SIDE OF THE GENE POOL!

THERE'S NOTHING LIKE THE HOLIDAYS TO FILL YOU WITH THOUGHTS OF YOUR FAMILY.

IT'S THE LAST WORK WEEK OF THE YEAR! ISN'T ANYONE DOING ANYTHING ??

CERTAINLY, MR. PINKLEY.

CHARLENE'S WORKING ON THE NUT LOG... MARK AND SUE ARE PLOWING THROUGH THE MUFFIN BASKET...

FRANK'S FINISHING OFF THE FROSTED SANTAS... MARCIA'S DIVING INTO THE BUCKET OF CARAMEL CORN... AND I'M ABOUT TO GO INTO A CLOSED-DOOR SESSION WITH THE CHOCOLATE-COVERED PRETZELS!

AT LAST! SOMEONE'S FINALLY PAYING ATTENTION TO SOMETHING THAT CAME FROM OUR CLIENTS!

Panel 1:
MERRY CHRISTMAS, CHARLENE! I HOPE YOU LIKE IT!

YOU GOT THIS FREE BY BUYING $50 OF MAKEUP FOR YOURSELF, CATHY. I SAW THE DISPLAY AT THE MALL.

Panel 2:
I KNOW YOU'VE BEEN WANTING A NEW MAKE-UP BAG!

BUT YOU GOT IT FREE BUYING SOMETHING FOR YOURSELF.

Panel 3:
IT'S FILLED WITH LITTLE LIPSTICKS AND MASCARAS! A $19.95 VALUE!!

I SPENT A MONTH MAKING YOU THIS ALBUM OF ALL THE SPECIAL TIMES WE'VE HAD TOGETHER.

Panel 4:
HOW QUICKLY WE GO FROM GIFT WITH PURCHASE TO GUILT WITH PURCHASE.

Panel 5:
I CAN'T INVITE ALEX HOME FOR CHRISTMAS BECAUSE WE'RE NOT THAT SOLID OF A COUPLE.

Panel 6:
WE'RE ENOUGH OF A COUPLE FOR MY PARENTS TO SPEND THE WEEK GRILLING ME ABOUT HIM, BUT NOT ENOUGH OF A COUPLE FOR HIM TO BE THERE AS PART OF OUR FAMILY.

Panel 7:
WE'RE ENOUGH OF A COUPLE FOR THERE TO BE QUESTIONS, OPINIONS AND ANALYSIS, BUT NOT ENOUGH OF A COUPLE FOR HIM TO BE PRESENT FOR ANY OF IT.

Panel 8:
SOME PEOPLE HAVE RELATIONSHIPS. I HAVE CONVERSATION STARTERS.

Panel 9:
SIMON AND I LEAVE FOR HAWAII IN TWO DAYS! I HAVE SO MUCH TO DO!

YOU?? I HAVE TO LOSE TEN POUNDS BEFORE MY MOTHER STARTS FORCE-FEEDING ME MASHED POTATOES!

Panel 10:
I HAVE TO GET MY HAIR CUT BEFORE SHE STARTS PULLING IT BACK IN A CLIP... I HAVE TO IRON AND MEND ALL MY CLOTHES BEFORE SHE STARTS FUSSING OVER THEM....

Panel 11:
WHY ARE YOU GETTING SO CRAZY, CATHY? YOUR PARENTS LIVE RIGHT HERE IN TOWN.

EASY FOR YOU TO SAY...

Panel 12:
YOU'RE ONLY FLYING 5,000 MILES. I'M DRIVING 20 YEARS BACK IN TIME.